Contemporary Indian English LITERATURE

In the Young Twenties of the 21st Century

Contemporary Indian English LITERATURE

In the Young Twenties of the 21st Century

Editor

Arsha. S. Pillai

AUTHORSPRESS

Worldwide Circulation through Authorspress Global Network
First Published in 2022
by
Authorspress
Q-2A Hauz Khas Enclave, New Delhi-110 016 (India)
Phone: (0) 9818049852
E-mail: authorspressgroup@gmail.com
Website: www.authorspressbooks.com

Contemporary Indian English Literature:
In the Young Twenties of the 21st Century

ISBN 978-93-5529-084-7

Printed in India at Kensington Press

To
Amma And Darsu

Preface

When surgeon turned entrepreneur Sake Dean Mahomed chose English to write his travel experiences in 1793; it heralded a new era in Indian literature. 'The Travels of Dean Mahomed' is now judged as the first Indian book published in English. By default, he has become the father of Indian English literature. Though its history is relatively short, Indian English writings have come a long way, from nonfiction works such as political essays and biographies to original fiction that matches global standards. Apart from their high literary standards, most Indian English writings are now reflecting the ground-level realities of India in a better way than those of which appear in regional languages. Critical issues ranging from nationality, gender, identity, politics, faith, religion, secularism, subaltern existence and environment are finding a place in contemporary writings. Thus Indian English literature now is an extensive and diverse canvass. Now even regional level authors who write primarily in their mother tongues are trying to write in English. What's remarkable is the high representation of women in Indian English writings. While going through this collection of essays compiled by Arsha S Pillai, what's noticeable immediately is the transformation the Indian English literature has achieved over the years. It came a long way from the days of R K Narayan, Mulk Raj Anand and Raja Rao. This collection of essays is a clear reflection of the contemporary vibrance and vastness of Indian English literature. The book brings about a comprehensive platform where there is space for subjects ranging from love poetry to resistance literature. It conveys the magnificent diversity of Indian writings easily.

A set of authors have been analysed here, and this book explores the Indianness in their works in terms of the words they are using and the style they are pursuing. The Indian English publishing sector is now flooded with fiction and nonfiction of varying quality. The sector seems to have come of age. The authors introduced here hail from different backgrounds, and they write with emotions ranging from humour, courage, sarcasm and fury to create images that reflect the changing ethos of India's social life. Altogether, these contemporary authors widen the canvas of Indian writing in English by bringing different perspectives and genres in r literature. The book is a gateway to contemporary writings. It celebrates the success of Indian writers, especially women authors who are also significantly breaking into the field and making us proud of their beautiful writings. The editor deserves appreciation for doing such commendable work, which brings about a new feel and aesthetics. I am introducing this book to readers sans borders for wider appreciation and critical analysis with extreme privilege and happiness.

K.A. Shaji

(South India based developmental journalist)

Acknowledgement

Thanks to:

Dr. M.N. Parasuraman
Dr. Indu B
Dr. George Koshy
Dr. Chitra V.R.
Dr. Rakesh Babu M
Dr. Sreepriya R
Dr. S.K. Prathap
Kaikasi V.S
Ms. Lekshmi R.
Vishnu M Vijayakumar
Ms Siva Sanm
Abhinaya A
K.A. Shaji
Adarsh S.Pillai

Special Thanks to:

Nidhi Kumari
Sudharshan Kcherry

Contents

CHAPTER 1

The Geography of Love in *Like Blood on the Bitten Tongue* by Akhil Katyal

Aiswarya Thara Bhai Anish

From times immemorial, love has been a central theme in innumerable works of literature. Poetry beholds love and its conjuration of longing, loss and lust remain one of the most written and re-written forms of emotions; with each writer gaining a new perspective, each period weaving new insights on the way the *Homo sapiens* perceives and practices love. Akhil Katyal's *Like Blood on the Bitten Tongue* is a testimony to the practice of love, as it shatters the notions of heteronormativity and its tentacles shadowing the annals of homosexual love.

According to Judith Butler, 'the binary relation between culture and nature promotes a relationship of hierarchy in which culture freely 'imposes' meaning on nature'[1]. Katyal's poem titled *'Aligarh'* is a melancholic address to Dr. Ramachandra Siras where the poet mournfully looks at the nights the professor would have spent in hurtful solitude where he must have "felt the loneliness like a drip" after being suspended from the University alleging gross misconduct. Dr. Siras' house was broken into and he was captured on camera being intimate with a man – a 'gross misconduct' that he paid for with his life, in 2010, a day before his suspension was repealed by the authorities. Katyal's words draw parallels with the life he leads and the one Dr. Siras has led, asking

> What did you say, Dr Siras,
> When you looked for that house
> In Durga Wadi?

Katyal's question presents the dilemma of the unmarried, gay bachelor having to hide his identity to 'draw respect from the right surname' of 'teacher', his profession a shroud protecting a harrowing secret, to which Katyal asks 'What gives us this respect, Dr Siras,/this contract with water?'. Even the home where one puts the shroud down is violated, and with each pressing question of the landlord the poet says he will 'try and hide my feeling small/under my feet'.

Throughout *Like Blood on the Bitten Tongue*, Katyal makes his concerns of the homophobic realities of the space he has called home. A series of poems such as *'I want to 377 you so bad'* written in 2013, five years before Article 377 punishing sexual acts against the 'order of nature' was decriminalised in India, speaks about the aspirations of a gay man being who wants to "break laws/ with you in bed and in streets and parks". The poem's fluidic nature and its sense of urgency imitate the unveilings of a private moment – a desire that is doomed to break laws, it is as much an enjambment of unspent desire as it is of just rage at being criminalised in society, for being merely human. The 2014 poem *'Girl, when you'* picks up where the former left off, the poet's rage now collected, taunts the heterosexual acts of love that he patronisingly says, know(s) it feels like heaven, you too violate 377". Katyal targets the cultural matrix that prevents the heterosexual couple from being criminalised and looks at the guidelines that govern the way in which society perceives sexual norms. He moulds the same words that prosecute 'the other' to mimic expletives and erotic double entendre, such as the use of the term *377* to represent a 'criminal' act of love.

One of the striking features of Katyal's poems that revolve around the idea of love is its temporality. For Katyal, love is transient, shifting between cities and towns and in that process stereotyping them. The way in which Katyal moulds his lovers is by comparing them to places, nestled in the heartlands of Delhi. For instance, *Like Blood on the Bitten Tongue* begins with a poem that tells us an unnamed lover is as "arrogant as a Chattarpur farmhouse" (Katyal). Their love is also an architectural anomaly, a juxtaposition aptly made to the imposing, posh houses of Chattapur as they hold hands "infrequently and uneasily/like Def Col and Kolta", letting us know that this troubled love is like an uneased neighbourhood, an uncomfortable appeasement of emotions. We see their geography of love settling down in Jangpura and Jangpura Extension, the lover's arrogance mitigating as their love blossoms "more breezily" before embracing with the ferocity of Najafgarh and kissing with the gentle serenity of Shalimar Bagh (Katyal).

The love that Katyal portrays is an exclusive kind of one, unravelling itself only to the one who has walked the streets of Delhi or lived in its proximity to feel the heat of its summer and the smell of its people, distancing itself from the outsider who stumbles across these street names with a foreigner's awe, perhaps like the relatable love nestled in an unrelatable land. There is also a pronounced sapience at the disillusionment of time and space at the height of temporality. For instance, in the poem *Near Eros Cinema, Jangpura Extension*, we see a conglomeration of different localities visualised in the everyday realities of the 'rickshaw-guy from Darbhanga' and the condescending 'aunty' who 'makes a मुंह (face)', the shop cleaner from Muzaffarpur watching the billboards with the "50 year old hero and a 20 year old heroine that he will woo"[2]. Despite such distinct notions of localities in observance, the poet tells us;

And I am walking with his
hands in mine, feelin' here-&-now
and also a no-where-in-particular. (Jangpura extension)

It is difficult to perceive the emotions the poet feels at this juncture, his sense of space diluted as his hands merge with that of his lover's, his visions more focused on the paraphernalia surrounding him than the subtle expression of love he is partaking in. The poet's hesitation in fully being at home with his lover reaches a pinnacle in the poem "तुम कोई मेट्रो स्टेशन होती" (If you were a metro station), where he tells us,

तो ज़रूर येल्लो लाइन पर	*You must have been*
'घिटोरनी' होती	*'Ghitorni' on the Yellow Line*
इससे कम दमदार नाम	*Any other name less authoritative*
तुम पर जचता ही नहीं	*than this would not have equalled you.*

He thus compares his lover to the imposing and well-connected Ghitorni village and goes on to say that no other name would have been apt for his lover, which makes the reader reminiscence about the arrogance of his lover who both intimidates and enthrals Katyal so much that he writes he is afraid of coming there, that he is meek.

तुम्हारे मेरे बीच ये पूरी दिल्ली है	*The whole of Delhi parts us away from each other,*
इसलिए आने से डरता हूँ	*so I am afraid of coming there*
थोड़ा मीक हूँ	*I am indeed, a little meek.*

In *'Five Things I noticed in the 1807 map of Delhi'*, Katyal takes us on a history lesson, noting down his observations of Delhi fifty years before the Revolt of 1857; before the walled city would be 'bayoneted on the spot'. Despite the map's scale being 'emotionally accurate', the poet observes that the place where he and his lover met are not on the map, a casual observation on a numbered list. This sublunary love that weaves in and out, right in the middle of concrete places speaks of the abstract nature of their romance, everywhere and the nowhere, discernible yet complex.

Works Cited

1. Judith Butler, Judith Butler, *Gender Trouble: Feminism and the Subversion of Identity* (New York: Routledge, 1990), 24.
2. Katyal, Akhil. *Like Blood on the Bitten Tongue:* Delhi Poems (p. 28). Kindle Edition.

CHAPTER 2

Subverted Epic Tales in Indian Literature through the Works of Kavita Kane

Hanna Isath N

"A classic is a book that has never finished saying what it has to say..."

(Calvino 128)

Calvino's wise words about classical works delineate the revered canon and its abilities in ushering mankind into the invaluable world of literature. These words elucidate not just the features of a classical work but the study of literature itself. Literature has to some extent captured the eventful human life and the perennial experiences through a medium that surpass the ephemerality of man.

The literary outputs are unpredictable and are largely based on several factors that are prone to frequent variations like social, political and economic measures. Literature in general and Indian Writings are no less different in their transformation and progress. It has truthfully documented the ups and downs and touched upon a pre-independent and post-independent Indian taste and style.

While the appeal of urban realism evident in the works of Rabindranath Tagore, Mulk Raj Anand, Bankim Chandra Chattopadhyay, Munshi Premchand, Raja Rao etc. gradually lost its traction, Indian writing have entered into a new phase with the obvious infusion of magic realism like in the works of Salman Rushdie, Arundhati Roy, Chitra Banerjee Divakaruni, Vikram Chandra, the diasporic tales with postcolonial fallout like in the works of Jhumpa Lahiri, Bharati Mukherjee, Kiran Desai.

Perspective Writing which was perfected by Anand Neelakantan is yet another innovative writing style that opened up a treasure trove of stories that focuses on retelling the epic. The cliched villains who adorn the age-old epics are portrayed in a different light enhancing their stature and appeal in the eyes of the common man. Kavita Kane, Amish Tripathi, Dr Devdutt Pattanaik have also contributed to this writing style and have greatly excelled in giving the epics a modern twist.

The latest addition to the growing trend in this field is the emergence of novels that showcases the life of the marginalised and subjugated characters. Supplanting the mainstream heroes, unheard voices, denigrated figures and mutilated bodies take the limelight. Dalit writings that delineate the segregation, afflictions and survival of one of the most apartheid sections in India, the Dalits, occupies an inevitable place in Indian literature.

The burgeoning field of sexual studies has made its way into Indian writings too wherein the discourse veneers to the LGBTQ+ congregation. The rising homophobic tendencies and fear of the other sexual orientations call for attention and hence a spurt of novels on the same theme is not a surprise. Such novels play a pivotal role in restructuring the conventional beliefs that formulate the patriarchal strictures prevalent in India.

Each au courant writing technique not only entertains the masses but also nurture and enlighten the sceptical minds of society. Literature, a subjective medium that uses emotions and feelings to communicate sprints ahead in awakening the restless and tepid intellect of the people. The literati could be the subject of ridicule, controversies and even be the potential targets of hate crimes for the revolutionary messages they impart through their novels. Despite these ordeals, books become the be-all and end-all of a person's life. He grows, moulds and thrives with the knowledge he acquires not just from his surroundings but the numerous fictional and non-fictional protagonists that he meets on the way.

Kavita Kane born on August 5, 1966, in Pune is an Indian novelist, journalist and scriptwriter. She has carved a name for herself in the genre of retellings of the epics and is one of the proficient writers of Mythology fiction. She specialises in Indian myth especially with a profound sense of the great Indian epics like the Mahabharata and the Ramayana. All her works are primarily based on epics and are noted for the presence of powerful female protagonists.

Kane was successful in introducing feministic ideals in the oldest literary genre that is mythology. Incorporating feminism in antique pieces takes great courage and intellect. Such a mode would be subversive and transgressive at the same time. Kane is a die-hard lover of myths and legends that prompted her to try a hand at creative writing which was a definite swerve from her journalistic pieces. In an interview with *The Indian Express*, Kane speaks about her affinity to myths, "I always believed that mythology can be a huge canvas for contemporary thought. It is not telling us some old tales, as so carelessly assumed, of Gods and Goddesses, but of Man and his follies and fallacies."

Kane defines mythology as "a literary device to portray contemporary issues and sensibilities" and strongly opines that "mythology should make you think, not judge." The power of perspective plays an important role in her novels. The secondary characters are more complex and detailed than her protagonist which shows how Kane prioritise the marginalised caricatures in her novels.

Kane's breakthrough novel is *The Karna's Wife: The Outcast Queen* (2013). The novel portrays the epic character of Karna through the eyes of Uruvi. Through the novels, we see Karna not just as Uruvi's husband but as a legendary warrior, belittled Sudra, loyal friend to Duryodhan and the hidden brother to the Pandavas in a completely different light.

It was soon succeeded by novels like *Sita's Sister* (2014) depicts the story of Urmila, Sita's sister and Lakshmana's wife. Kane describes this novel as Urmila's "own private legend" and a story unheard by any as the name Ramayana is equivalent to Ram and Sita. *Sita's Sister* elucidates the much-neglected character of Urmila who could be considered as the perfect subverted specimen in an epic with her keen observation, sharp words and quintessential boldness.

Menaka's Choice (2015) was Kane's third novel which focuses on the story of Menaka and her relationship with Vishwamitra. The novel portrays a different version of Menaka in stark contrast to the traditional seductress feminine figure. *Menaka's Choice* provides the outlet for the famous character of Menaka who proves that her existence is not just justified as a femme fatal but as an individual who strongly questions her relationships with the various individuals who shaped and influenced her life.

Lanka's Princess (2016) soon followed which portrays the story of Ravana's infamous sister Suparnakha. The novel surprises everyone with the unexpected choice of character, Suparnakha, who is not just the privileged sister to the epic villain of Ramayan but a feminine figure who is as stately and divine as Sita herself reveals as the character greatly misconstrued to be drunk in revenge and hateful to the core but in reality, was a figure truly abandoned in the light of her brothers quest for power. Suparnakha showcases her grit and gumption even during the lowest periods of her life as misery and misfortune swamps her life and homeland but never truly breaking her.

The Fisher Queen's Dynasty (2017) introduces the storyline of the grand matriarch of the Kuru family, Satyavati. The novel envisages the trials and tribulations undergone by Satyavati, a princess with the fishy redolence, and her quest for power and grandeur of the Kuru family with her quick thinking, stunning willpower and dominant personality wrapped by the ecstasy of motherhood.

Ahalya's Awakening (2019) questioned the judgemental society and the notion of infidelity and its repercussions on the female gender. The novel delves into the eponymous protagonist Ahalya as a Künstlerroman stylistic narration wherein Ahalya is enlightened through the study of Vedas. Ahalya is soon exposed to the experiences of sexual awakening and the succeeding events leading to infidelity and penalty shapes the novel that serves not merely as a documentation of the struggles of a minor epic character but as a cautionary tale for the contemporary woman who fights for her rights and responsibilities.

Kane's latest and her seventh novel titled Saraswati's Gift (2021) takes on the tale of the Goddess of art, knowledge and music, Saraswati, and her relationship with the Triumvirate Hindu Gods. Saraswati despite being a divine figure widely revered and worshipped by devotees is no stranger to the mainstream exclusion usually meted out to indomitable independent figures in the society. The novel demystifies the Goddess from an unfamiliar perspective thereby prompting a profound study and distinct tale on the Goddess.

Kavita Kane has inevitably broken the stereotypical and cliched feminine characters and has moulded them into fiercely independent and self-loving minds. Kavita stresses the importance of mythology in an interview with the Hindu wherein she states that:

> If myths reflect the socio-cultural ethos of earlier times, they can also be used to contemporise those same issues in today's world. Actually, nothing has changed. Love, rivalry, disappointment, war, anger, greed… all of

these emotions still exist. There's a chance of an alternative perspective by looking at the epics through the women and minor characters at that.

This excerpt tries to analyse how Kavita Kane uses the story of the epic especially Mahabharata to weave a narrative that shoes light on a minor or neglected character like that of Uruvi, the Princess of Pukeya in her debut novel The Karna's Wife: The Outcast Queen. This novel despite being her debut enthrals the public with its focus on critical notions on the subverted characters, inverted epic tales, distorted matchmaking procedures and the devious, cynical and hypocritical regal life. The novel abounds with rich characters with surprising stories unheard of in a unique style engrossing the readers and at the same time evoking the analytical fervour of the public. The novel succeeds in delineating each of these aspects through the character of Uruvi, an unsung heroine in the epic who finally received the appreciation and exposure she befits. The novel in a way brings to the forefront the unheard yet vivacious and intellectual heroine Uruvi who steals the thunder from her valiant husband Karna designated as the greatest hero of all times.

History has been kind to Karna and numerous works were written praising the valour, loyalty and magnificence of the character. Kane uses Karna to prise out the unexpected but charming character of Uruvi. In the novel, Uruvi is described as:

> Uruvi was the only daughter of the sixth King of Pukeya, the erudite Vahusha and Queen Shubra; an heiress to her father's legacy, his intelligence, and her mother's flaming beauty. Slender and petite, her loveliness was distracting, speciously masking her incisive wit. Though the burning fire in her eyes, the warmth of her smile, and the passion with which she articulated her thoughts were enticing, she was too spirited to be restrained, too proud to be cautious, and far too forthright to think of the consequences of her actions. She had a charming candour, a blithe audacity steeled with a stubborn resilience, which many admired but few appreciated. (Kane 14)

> Uruvi excelled in music and arts and had an innate taste and shined in horse riding. Uruvi also found her calling in healing and soon became hope to the wounded and bloodied bodies on the battlefield. "While girls of her age were groomed to become dainty princesses, Princess Uruvi saddled her horse each morning to ride to the gurukul where she spent the day immersed in the world of medicinal herbs and other remedies"(Kane 26).

Despite the repeated warnings from her father that "'There are four examples of bad men these days, the dushta chathushtayam,' he said. 'One is Shakuni, Duryodhana's maternal uncle. The second is

Duryodhana himself. The third is the malicious Dushasana. And the fourth, sadly, is Karna." (Kane 32) Uruvi becomes the victim of her hearts' longing and eventually falls madly in love with Karna the first time she ever sees him afar. This seals Uruvi's fate as the wife of one of the most misunderstood, belittled Suta Putra Karn. Uruvi tries to break the stereotypes but to no avail yet her recalcitrant attitude and her strong morals make her enviable to the Vedic society.

The novel begins with Uruvi's dream wherein she gets a glimpse of her mysterious man who later turns out to be her husband. Uruvi is shown to have the power of foreseeing the future and the dreams appear again at various parts of the novel at the most crucial juncture in Uruvi's life even when it does not overtly help her overcome the trials and tribulations in her life. Her swayamwara was the perfect antithesis to the matchmaking ideologies prevalent during the times. Uruvi was born a princess through her nuptials to Karna was relegated to the lowest rungs of the caste hierarchy. She was jeered at by her kith and kin except for her parents. As a princess, she was bound to choose a Kshatriya warrior in the likes of Arjuna but she surprised everyone by marrying a Suta prince that too who has already married to Vrushali, a Suta, and a father to her children.

Uruvi's affable demeanour and her profound love for Karna made it easier for the princess to adapt easily to her new lifestyle at Anga. Uruvi got along with everyone especially Vrushali and her in-laws with the sole exception of Karna's best friend Duryodhan. Uruvi along with other members of Karna's family strongly believed that the Kaurava prince was the root cause of all evil that has befallen Karna and yet to befall him. Uruvi decides to take the bull by its horn and tries to persuade Karna to forego his friendship with Duryodhan but to no avail. This friendship is undisputedly the time tested and most endearing of all relationships between two individuals ironically so different in beliefs but similar in their mutual love, respect and loyalty. Uruvi vehemently hated Duryodhana and felt strongly that Karna was just a tool and powerful pawn in the hands of Duryodhana. Later Uruvi retracts this belief by stating that "Their friendship will be their downfall, but I admit, it's a bond that is strong and everlasting." (339)

Uruvi's stinging remarks at Karna in the light of what happened to Draupadi shows how Uruvi acts as the conscious keeper of Karna prompting him to introspect and calling out his actions based on friendship. She calls spade a space and is not afraid of speaking her mind even to the great patriarch Bhishma. Kunti is considered to be Uruvi's Godmother and the princess is widely loved and respected by everyone. Though fazed by Draupadis' feelings for quite some time Uruvi remains steadfast in her belief in Karna and goes to the extent of idolising her husband. Uruvi is unlike the normal epic characters but emerges as a woman of grit and compassion with tinges of rebellion at the face of criticisms and harangues.

Uruvi might be Kane's first subverted character in the long list of other epic figures like Urmila, Ahalya, Menaka and others but Uruvi imposes her presence like no other. Passed off as a minor figure in the epic Kane embellished Uruvi to the stature she deserves and hopes to be remembered among the tales of tall warriors in the epic.

Work Cited

Calvino, Italo. *The Uses of Literature.* Pantheon Books, 1999.

Kane, Kavita. *The Karna's Wife: The Outcast Queen*, 2013.

Kane, Kavita. "The Kavita Kane interview: Why Feminism in Indian mythology matters today". *The New Indian Express*, 04 November 2017.

Kane, Kavita. "Through another pair of eyes: A chat with author Kavita Kane". *The Hindu*, 05 November 2020.

CHAPTER 3

Bruised Minds: An Exploration of Traumatic Overtones in Githa Hariharan's *Fugitive Histories*

Athira S. S.

Indian Literature in English which spans almost all genres of literature like fiction, non-fiction, poetry and drama refers to the works written in English by Indian authors whose mother-tongue is one of the regional languages in India. English is a global language that acts as a medium for many writers to gain proper acknowledgement for their works. Indian Literature in English has attained an independent status among world literature through its portrayal of wide range of themes such as Indian culture, tradition, social values and Indian history. It bears an unavoidable stamp of Indianness and expresses a shared tradition, cultural experience and Indian heritage.

Githa Hariharan is a celebrated Indian author who had marked her indelible presence in the realm of the Indian literary arena with her works that offer a realistic rendering of the life of Indian women. Her famous works include *The Thousand Faces of Night* which won the Commonwealth Writers Prize for Best First Book in 1993, the short story collection *The Art of Dying*, the novels *The Ghost of Vasu Master*, *When Dreams Travel*, *In Times of Siege* and *Fugitive Histories.* Gita Hariharan uses her works as a medium to portray the prominent issues that are prevalent in our society. Her works offer a detailed study of the varying psychological condition of her characters as to show how the dominant societal issues affect them emotionally and physically. The theory of trauma also gains significance in some of her works as they portray how some shocking troublesome experiences create traumatic disturbances in the psyche of individuals.

The concept of trauma originally developed in the domain of medicine and psychology crossed boundaries between various fields of study and gained relevance in the area of literature in the mid-twentieth century. The term trauma, originated from Greek generally refers to a physical injury or a wound. It also refers to a severe emotional shock caused by an extremely painful event that may lead to psychological damage. Trauma can be identified both as an individual and a collective phenomenon. Individual trauma acts as a shock to the psyche of the individual as it happens all of a sudden leading to a critical traumatic disorder. Collective trauma occurs when a particular group of people undergo a certain traumatic event together.

Collective trauma is different from individual trauma as it is embedded in the memory of the group and creates a bond and feeling of unity among these groups of people. Sociologist Kai Erikson differentiated between Individual and Collective Trauma as

> By individual trauma I mean a blow to the psyche that breaks through one's defenses so suddenly and with such brutal force that one cannot react to it effectively...by collective trauma, on the other hand, I mean a blow to the basic tissues of social life that damages the bond attaching people together and impairs the prevailing sense of communality. (153-154)

Some instances of collective traumatic situations may include wars, natural disasters, pandemics, and terrorism. These types of traumatic occurrences may lead to a series of physical, psychological and societal consequences that in turn will disrupt the very existence of the community.

Githa Hariharan's prestigious novel *Fugitive Histories* published in the year 2009 interweaves the stories of three women Mala, Sara and Yasmin who are all the victims of trauma in some way or other. The author has set the novel in the backdrop of the Godhra riot in the year 2002 which has resulted in the death of a large number of Hindus and Muslims. The novel opens with Mala, a widow searching through the sketchbook collection of her dead husband Asad. Mala Vaidhyanathan who was born and brought up in a traditional south Indian Brahmin family marries Asad, a Muslim settled in Mumbai, against her family's wish. Even though Asad belongs to a traditional Muslim family, he is a secular activist who hates religious identities. They have two children, Samar and Sara. Samar is a Software Engineer who plans to leave for America whereas Sara works with an

NGO in Mumbai. Sara along with her friend Nina plans for a documentary based on the massacre followed by the Godhra riot in 2002. She visits Ahmadabad and meets the victims of the communal violence and Yasmin, a seventeen-year-old girl is prominent among them. Gita Hariharan brings out various aspects of individual and collective trauma in this novel through the portrayal of characters who were suffering due to the indelible scars marked by the horrific events that affected them.

In the novel *Fugitive Histories*, the Godhra riot of the year 2002 serves as the major instance of traumatic troubles for the community of Muslims. The uprising broke out with the burning of Sabarmati Express on February 27, 2002 which caused the death of 58 Hindus returning from Ayodhya including women and children. This paved way for the violent outbreak in which the minority population of Muslims in Gujarat were brutally massacred. Muslim families were burnt alive in their homes, their shops and businesses were also set on fire. Even women and children were not left alone since they were brutally gang raped and killed. The unforgettable pain caused by the devastating riot is portrayed vividly in the novel by Githa Hariharan.

The aftermath of the horrific events following the riot was so harsh on the lives of ordinary people. Githa Hariharan describes a woman named Zahida who was deeply affected by the outbreak that she stopped talking after that incident. "May be Zahida-khala's afraid that if she opens her mouth she may scream again. Maybe that's all she can really remember: something is happening; somethings are happening; and she is screaming, screaming" (158). The violent massacre which was part of the riot was deeply embedded in the inner psyche of the community that they are unable to get rid of these memories from their mind. These memories always create a kind of fear in them and it affects even their struggle for survival. Another woman named Mariam explains: "It means our men were killed, it means our mothers and sisters and daughters were raped. It means we saw it happening. Our people were grilled like meat. I saw it with my own eyes. The bodies piled up. Everything was over in a flash". (159). Along with the brutal killing and murder that happened before them the womenfolk of the community became victims as well as witnesses of cruel gang rapes also. They were subjected to extreme cruelty amidst these violent uprising. Zainab says about her sister who lives among them as a victim of gang rape who was unable to overcome the trauma of that particular day as she cries out loudly whenever the memory comes to her.

The plight of young women is more evident when Zulekha recalls the events of those days as "Those girls were screaming, they were begging us to remove the stumps of wood that had been pushed into them. Each one was crying," Me first, remove mine first." I'll never forget their screams. Even now, when I tell you this, my blood boils" (160). The womenfolk of the community were subjected to extreme kind of brutality amidst the violent uprising and those terrific memories haunt them continuously. In the case of Yasmin also it had a devastating effect since her thigh which has a scar left by the attackers throbs whenever she was reminded of those difficult days.

A person affected by trauma will be in a condition of numbness. For a traumatised individual the past incident will often jump into the present and then it will shift back and forth in time and place so that the traumatised person cannot realise whether it is reality or fantasy. Memory serves as a major factor in intensifying the traumatic effects in an individual. In the case of Yasmin, trauma is rooted mainly in two things: the memories of the violent massacre and also her memory of her happy life with her brother. Yasmin is the most significant character in the novel through whom the shocking aspects of the riot are revealed. Yasmin is a seventeen-year-old girl who struggles hard to get rid of her memories regarding the troublesome past. She was leading a very happy life along with her parents and brother Akbar. Everything turned upside down when one day her brother went missing and all of a sudden a group of people set her father's shop on fire and also one among them tried to molest her. Though she could escape rape, the memories of that day and the plight of other women around her prevents her from sleeping peacefully. This incident had created an indelible mark on her psyche that she became a girl who was afraid of silly things. It is written as

> Yasmin's thigh throbs: it's only a scar, there's blood running under the skin, there's no piece of wood jamming up its flow. But how strange it is, being hated. It makes old scars pain all over again. And how strange it is to hate. It opens up the old wound, it makes it throb so you think it's a fresh one, you have been wounded all over again. (161)

The knowledge that she cannot see her brother again keeps on traumatising her. She finds comfort in her secret hope that her brother will return one day and with this belief, she finds comfort in his photograph and textbooks. Everyday after the riot Yasmin lives in fear as she says:

> It means running, hiding, keeping her racing heart quiet and still because there's someone after her and he may hear it. Someone or many someones. They may have tilaks on their foreheads, trishuls in their hands. Trishuls, or swords, pipes, rods, hockey sticks. Anything that can hit or cut. (123)

Asad is an indirect victim of the shocking events of the communal riot. The strong and liberal man in Asad cannot bear the bloodshot and violence of the riot. It affected him mentally and gradually it leads to the deterioration of his physical condition. Even though his artistic productivity increases, he changes completely as he feels a kind of dejection in his life. He finds it very hard to cope with the shock of traumatic events that affect his life and it ends in his death. Mala experiences certain instances of traumatic struggle after the death of her husband Asad. She searches through the sketchbooks left behind by Asad and it brings back her memories of the past leaving her with sleepless nights. Even though she asserts to her children that she will manage to live after Asad's death it is troublesome for her to spend time in her bedroom with memories of Asad.

Collective trauma has a devastating effect on the entire existence of the community since it affects them psychologically and physically. It can also be intergenerational since the people who are unable to cope with the shock may transfer it to the next generation also. But in this novel Gita Hariharan beautifully portrays how the womenfolk of the society tries to overcome the disturbing effects of trauma by keeping in mind the safe future of their children. They work hard in-order to present their children with a bright future. Inspite of all the traumatic troubles they need to live again for a better future. So to a certain extent these people were able to overcome the horrific effects of trauma which was caused by the communal riot that shattered the very existence of their living.

The novel *Fugitive Histories* is a wonderful portrayal of the troubling effects of trauma as an individual and collective phenomenon. The novel offers a brilliant portrayal of the effects of trauma on the lives of characters. The collective trauma finds its manifestation in the lives of the Muslim community especially the womenfolk whereas Yasmin, Asad and Mala were the victims of individual trauma. The most admiring thing regarding the characters in this novel is that they were able to break free from the shackles of trauma through their mental strength. Yasmin finds solace in her prayers and also in the notebooks left behind by her brother. It is through studying better and gaining admission to a college that she escapes her fear of the world. The community of Muslims who were the victims of the communal riot were also able to find a way out from their traumatic struggles with their hope for a better future for their children. Mala also finds a way out from her troubled mindset by doing proper funeral rites for Asad by dropping his palette knife and paintbrush in the pond. In this novel, Githa Hariharan beautifully portrays the varying aspects of trauma in the characters and also she was able to portray how far they were able to escape from the devastating effect of trauma as to lead a successful life.

Work Cited

Caruth, Cathy. *Unclaimed Experiences: Trauma, Narrative and History*. Johns Hopkins University Press, 1996.

Erikson, Kai. T. *Everything in its Path*. Simon and Schuster, 1976.

Hariharan, Githa. *Fugitive Histories*. Penguin Books, 2009.

Hirschberger, Gilad. "Collective Trauma and the Social Construction of Meaning." *Frontiers in Psychology*, 10 Aug. 2018.

www.frontiersin.org/articles/10.3389/fpsyg.2018.01441/

La Capra, Dominick. *Writing History, Writing Trauma*. Johns Hopkins University Press, 2001.

CHAPTER 4

When the Snow Turns Red: The Tales of Unheard from the Perspective of a Native

Nidhi Kumari

> "There's really no such thing as the 'voiceless'. There are only the deliberately silenced, or the preferably unheard"
>
> Arundhati Roy

Resistance literature have gained grounds through the writings on Kashmir, North east and Dalit writings in independent India. It expresses the angst and becomes a tool of the powerless to voice and forms a symbol of rebellion and expression. It paves way for the reader to understand the forgotten people of the land and identify them. Kashmir is always crowned as the land of desire and through resistance literature the marginalised voices are heard aloud. The new writing about the land has not seen Kashmir in isolation instead we have writers who focus on the rich tradition of Kashmir, conflicts and its present state through multiple dimensions. There are many narratives of the same story from both the outsider and the natives, and the voices of the latter often resembles as resistance within resistance writing.

Mirza Waheed is one such voice of the contemporary era, who was born and brought up in Srinagar, Kashmir and now lives in London. At the age of eighteen, he moved to study English literature at the University of Delhi and for four years he worked as a journalist and editor in the city. In 2001, he came to London to join the BBC's Urdu Service, where he now works as an editor. Author of three novels and many other essays, his works have been appreciated for giving a new perspective to the themes that were dealt in the mainstream. Most of his work focuses on the issues of his native land, thus he becomes the voice of his community. Through his works he tries to bring the issues of the land into limelight from the perspective of the natives. His works mostly deal with the theme of conflicts both external and internal caused by the happenings as well as the choices taken by an individual. He is a recipient of the Hindu Literary award 2019.

The Collaborator, his debut novel, is the first fictional narrative dealing with Kashmiri issue written by a native published in 2011. It narrates the story of coming of age of the narrator which is juxtaposed with the dramatic turn of events in Kashmir. The novel is divided into three parts: Now and Then, Then and Now. It is set in a village near LOC, border dividing India and Pakistan. The novel shows how the paradise is transformed into a graveyard where thousands lie without a proper burial. The conflict between the two nations claiming Kashmir disturbs the peace of land which forces people to leave their own homeland is portrayed in the novel.

His second novel, *The Book of Gold Leaves*, a slow burn love story of Rohi and Faiz was published in 2015. It is a love story between a Sunni and a Shi'ite in troubled 1990's Kashmir. Through this the writer provides insights into the class conflict within the Kashmiri Muslims, it also talks about the beauty of Kashmir and how the natural disaster and other political issues scars it. This book is a reflection of the blend of art and culture of Kashmir, as well as on the ecological changes happening there.

His third novel *Tell Her Everything* was released in 2019. It is the story of a father who is preparing to reveal his own unsavoury past to the now-grown daughter that he sent away to boarding school as a small child. It is a monologue and represents the internal conflict of the father due to the choices he had made in his professional life which were against the ethics of the profession.

He writes in the most delicate manner that makes his lines lyrical embedded in emotions. He gives vivid descriptions of the history, Kashmiri landscape, innocent passion and romance and the intriguing violence too. The tone of melancholy precedes in his narrative within the colourful land of Kashmir. The fear of the events is grippled into the mind of the reader and it sustains evoking the emotions. The juxtaposition of the subtle and harsh, unsheltered and sheltered and the realities and vagaries are depicted.

Indian society like any other society has faced a lot of conflicts from caste, class, creed, sex, community to nation as a whole. The partition of India and Pakistan after independence had led to various political conflicts, which traumatised people. Kushwant Singh has described the separation, tragic experience and the nostalgia of Sikhs who were forced to leave their homeland in Pakistan. Since partition, communal riots have been recurrent in India; various versions of these have been narrated. Religious sentiments in India have always been manipulated to cause communal riots like Gujarat riots and communal riots happening often in Uttar Pradesh. Amidst these, the external conflicts, especially war like situations with neighbouring countries has increased tension in the bordering states, because of which the army has been deployed in those areas. But military insurgency and militant invasion in Kashmir and North-eastern states have disturbed the normal life of people. Though many outsiders have written about these issues, the writers like Thangjam Ibopishak Singh, Janice Pariat, Rahul Pandita, Mirza Waheed became the prominent voices of these regions, from the perspective of a native, the one who has seen and experienced it closely.

Mirza Waheed strongly believes literature is a reflection of life and can help in understanding the society and it also acts as a medium to bring positive change. For him pen is mightier than sword and uses it profusely to make the world hear the unheard tales of Kashmir. In one of the interviews with the Hindu, Waheed says,

> "I am still angry with the Indian state for its actions in Kashmir and I think I have written a few times about how I feel about it all. Literature helps us make sense of ourselves and of our world, which is shaped by politics whether we like it or not, whether we acknowledge it or not. And, of course, literature sheds light on the world in a way no amount of instant news or social media can, it shakes the lid off the darker aspects of our world. Fiction, however, takes time to gestate, to ripen, if I may. Yes, I will write about it. In what form and shape, I do not know" (Waheed).

"If there is heaven on earth, it's here, it's here, it's here", this is what Amir-e-Khusru said about Kashmir. But with time, the paradise has turned into a hell, it has become a volatile and disputed territory. Now the thought of Kashmir brings images of battles, concentration camps, bomb blasts, bloodshed and many more that have tortured the land. The geographical location makes it a beautiful place and the crown of India but the same thing has made it a war place, more precisely a political gambit. Waheed in his works, brilliantly portrays this horrendous transition. In *The Book of Gold Leaves* like a papier-Mache artist he illustrates different shades of Kashmir bringing forth the vibrant and serene beauty. The lush green valley, meadows, clear streams and snow-clad mountains gives vivid pictures of the beauty and peaceful coexistence of natives. He also points out how the nature is an integral part of Kashmiri life and the biodiversity becomes a source of their livelihood. But after partition, the lives of natives changed and so the ecology of the place, the narrator of *The Collaborator* describes the present state of the land, where everyone must carry an identity card, army pickets can be found everywhere and mass disposal of dead bodies. The impact of armed conflict on the nature can be understood through the description of narrator in *The Collaborator*,

> The Pakistanis were pounding a mountain pass some distance away, the Indians were replying in kind. There would be blood, and sulphur, on the trees. Dark plumes of smoke would emerge from the green canopies. Pines, those majestic umbrella pines, would be broken, their spectacular dark green spreads turning to umbrellas of crumbling flame, smoke and ash. (Waheed, 104)

Mirza Waheed through his first two novels occasionally gives a glimpse of the beautiful valley, which is a thing of the past, using flashbacks which helps in recognising how the chaos and on-going violence has led to the ecological crisis.

The conflict in Kashmir is not new to India, instead it can be said as both the oldest as well as the newest. There will be hardly any month or year or even days since independence that Kashmir is not in the news. It is a volatile as well as a burning issue. The recent one being the withdrawal of article 370 which caused many political issues and recent attack of terrorists on the migrant workers as well as on the natives.

Kashmir shares its borders with three other countries, of which China and Pakistan have always claimed their ownership over the land. The war has been ongoing between Pakistan and India as well as China and India for this piece of land. The natives are the ones who are suffering the most and this struggle for survival amidst the war between two countries is the subject of Mirza Waheed's first novel *The Collaborator*. The sounds of the bullets have become the lullaby while seeing a dead body of someone from their own community has become a regular thing. They have been fed up with all these and want it to end once and for all, the narrator in the novel says, "Why can't they just have another war instead – a proper, proper war – and get it over with. This *ikka-duka gola baari*, this damned 'sporadic shelling on the LoC', I'm sick of it". (Waheed, 115)

Though the novel is a fiction it appears very close to reality. The narration by a native of the land gives it a touch of personal experience. This is a book with detailed melancholy of Kashmir and people residing there. It is a saga of innocence, loss, pain, and rebellion. The novel focuses on the people residing in the LOC, in a village called Nowgam. It depicts the changes that took place, which transformed a peaceful land into macabre. It speaks about a community called Gujjars, a group of nomads, who were settled in Nowgam, a village in Kashmir for fifty years, their exodus and life of the very few families that never left in the hope that one day everything will become normal. The story is narrated by the unnamed boy who is 19 years old, the son of the headman, who has now become the collaborator of the army without his own will. His work is to collect the possessions of the dead bodies deposited in the valley, especially their Id cards and weapons as the military adds this to their records. The same valley of yellow flowers where now dead bodies is dumped contains memories from his childhood. He says that the army has turned his valley into a putrid trench. The beauty of nature also finds its place in the narration, whenever the narrator shifts from past to present, he describes the changes that have come to his surroundings including nature.

The conversation between the captain and the narrator taking place in the novel throws light upon how the military actions takes place and how at times innocent people are picked up, killed, then they are disguised into militants, weapons are kept on their sides to take photographs and circulate to the media, when they get orders to do something from higher authorities. The ordinary and innocent lives are at stake, they are not valued. The book puts forward horrifying tales of the militants and the Indian Army when they deal with the locals, and also gives glimpses of atrocities suffered during interrogation.

The war like situations create trauma, and the people living there are in constant fear. It affects the children, women the most. "Ma's stories dried up some time ago" (Waheed 102) the narrator tells it many times, reflecting how women have succumbed to their interiors, there is no more life in them. He also gives an account of an incident when women from far away came to the grocery shop crying out for milk for their children who are left as there is no milk left in their bosom due to lack of food supplies and they also tell children are dying due to starvation. Not only this but it also hampers the education and schooling of the coming generations. There is a brief detail about the visit of militants to the village, how they exhibited their power and how they want to take control over everything.

The narrator who badly wanted from the beginning of the novel to give a proper burial to the dead bodies in the valley, at the end gathers the courage and burns them up, thus giving them dignified death. He is burning everything that is dumped in the graveyard and it is symbolic of the burning sensations in Kashmir. The fire cripples the life of the individuals residing in the land. The torture that the ordinary villagers have to suffer is immense. They are wounded, mutilated and killed. The cruelty and torture of the military and militants have to be suffered by the layman of the land. The village lies in the line of the border. They have to leave the land and build everything from the beginning. This reflects the life condition of the people and the sufferings that they have to endure. They just want peace; they don't want anything that has destroyed their land and this feeling is aptly put by narrator:

> To hell with this all, I think, to hell with them all, to hell with the Indians, to hell with the killer dogs they send here in their millions to prey on us, to hell with all this swarming Army here, to hell with the Pakistanis, to hell with the Line of Control, to hell with Kadian and his Mehrotra Sir, to hell with India, to hell with Pakistan, to hell with jihad, and to hell with, to burning, smouldering hell with everything! (Waheed, 256).

To live a dignified life and to have a dignified death is the right of every individual, but the people of the valley do not have both. The cross-border issue has taken up a lot of lives and also made the lives of the residents horrible. The natives of Kashmir live in a constant fear, there is violence all around. The chaos, coercion and bloodshed has disrupted their life. There is only curfew, their right to expression is taken away, any kind of resistance is dealt with force, the military insurgency has done only harm, their life has been made hell, they are silenced to death. The fear and devastation make the people of Kashmir abandon their roots and flee. But no one is ready to solve these issues and they are made to suffer for the political agenda of the higher authorities. These indigenous voices are not even heard in the mainstream media, they just focus on the manipulated data. The ground reality is heart wrenching and gruesome. Though it will be hard to recoup the loss, still there is a hope, which Waheed expresses through Roohi in *The Book of Gold Leaves*,

> There is still love left in this land, so what if this lake is blighted and the Jhelum stifled? One day they will heal. One day I will plant so many willows around the Dal's magic rings that no one can cut through to its heart with their dirty hands. You must think I consider the lake my own – 'she smiles at herself '– and the rivers and mountains, too. Well, aren't they yours as well, Faizå?' (Waheed,135).

Mirza Waheed as a writer uses his voice for the oppressed, to raise their concerns and bring their sufferings to the notice of the mainland and the world. He puts forward the other side of the story where he not only talks about the plight of the people but also about the biodiversity, thus he narrates the suffering of the land as a whole. Through his works he wants the issues to be addressed and resolved so that the hope of natives to live peacefully in their homeland becomes reality.

Works Cited

Gupta, R. K. "Trends in Modern Fiction", World Literature Today, vol. 68, no, 2, 1994. www.jstor.org/stable/40150154. Accessed on 1 September 2021.

Rather, Mohd Nageen. "Conflict of Kashmir: Perspectives from two novels: Mirza Waheed's *The Collaborator* and Paro Anand's *No Guns at My Sons Funeral*". International Journal of Research in all subjects in Multi languages, vol. 5, no. 2, February 2017. www.raijmr.com/ijrsml/Accessed on 8 September 2021.

Roy, Arundhati. *An Ordinary Person's Guide to Empire*. Penguin India, 2006.

Shameem, Basharat. "Approximating history and experience through fiction: A study of Mirza Waheed's The Collaborator". ResearchGate, vol. 2, no. 3, 2019, www.researchgate.net/publication/331715714. Accessed on 2 September 2021.

Waheed, Mirza. *The Collaborator*. Penguin Group, 2011.

Waheed, Mirza. *The Book of Gold Leaves*. Penguin Books. 2014.

Waheed, Mirza. "Literature sheds light on the world in a way no news can". sheds-light-on-the-world-in-a-way-no-news-can-mirza- waheed/.Accessed on 5 September 2021.

CHAPTER 5

Arundhathi Subramaniam: Leaving a Legacy through Spirituality and Performing Arts

Greeshma Syam

Poetry possesses the advantage of absorbing local folklore forms, adapting the rhythm of spoken language and also an ability to draw audience to an intimate, emotional space. Though poetry was neglected by publishers because of its lack of readership it is now gaining momentum mainly due to the upsurge of publishing houses from ardent poetry lovers. Moreover, the proliferation of literary festivals allows a space for poetry to be discussed thus managing active forms of participation and negotiating multilingual and plural literary field. Since the last few years poetry has been performed in public with initiatives of curators like Ranjit Hoskote, Satabdi Mishra, Sonnet Mondal, Ankita Shah, Mamta Sagar and Arundhathi Subramaniam. Ranjit Hoskote curated his first exhibition when he was twenty-five and from then on to curate twenty exhibitions of contemporary Indian as well as international art. Satabdi Mishra curates Walking Book Fairs, a mobile book venture along with Akshaya Routray. Sonnet Mondal launched an international poetry festival in the city of Kolkata named The Chair Poetry Evenings. Similarly, Ankita Shah does performances of her poetry and Mamta Sagar has curated An Exhibition of Poetry in Piacenza, Italy. "Poetry is language longing to leap off a page", said Arundhathi Subramaniam echoing her efforts to do the same in an interview given to *The Hindu* (Zachariah).

Arundhathi Subramaniam who was born in 1973 in the city of Coimbatore, Tamil Nadu is a highly acclaimed Indian poet, writer, curator, translator, journalist writing in English. The author has to her credit twelve poetry collections including anthologies and six prose works. Subramaniam is one among the founding advisors of 'The (Great) Indian Poetry Collective', Head of *Dance and Chauraha*; a well-known inter-arts forum, a curator for classical dance at the National Centre for the Performing Arts in Mumbai and has been the Editor of the Indian domain of the *Poetry International Web*. The experience of living in the hustle and bustle of city life in Bombay and New York along with her knowledge in philosophy and mythology helps in the treatment of dealing with universal themes in her works. Therefore, she has struck a wonderful balance by grounding in the local traditions and spiritualities, especially the Bhakti movement while at the same time denying to belong to a particular culture or tradition.

Poetry Collections and Appearances in Anthologies

Arundhathi Subramaniam's poetry deals with the cultural and philosophical reflections of life. The sensuality of poetry and ambivalence of poetic language has fascinated the poet. The writer who is both a poet and translator has found constant inspiration in the works of A.K. Ramanujan and Arun Kolatkar. Wallace Stevens, T.S.Eliot, Tukaram, Denise Levertov, Basho, Adrienne Rich and Pablo Neruda are poets that have influenced her writing. She writes about existential themes like quest, gender politics, vulnerability, sacred journeys, identity, love, belonging and unbelonging in her works. Subramaniam's first collection of poetry *On Cleaning Bookshelves* published in 2001 is about rewriting the literary canon. The poet imagines small conversations with past writers. One of her early poems 'Amoeba' got into this exuberant collection. The second poetry collection, *Where I Live* (2005) explores ambivalences of being a woman and a Third World citizen. The theme of belonging and her love for the city of Mumbai is evident in her poems. The third book, *Confronting Love: Poems* is an anthology of forty-six contemporary Indian poets writing on love which Subramaniam co-edited with Jerry Pinto in 2005. In this anthology, poets writing in English convey the multiple shades of love and try to strike a balance between art and heart in dealing with the most beloved theme of poets over centuries. *Where I Live: New and Selected Poems* (2009) combines her first and second collections, *On Cleaning Bookshelves* and *Where I Live* with a selection of new work. This collection brings in her interest towards the sacred along with mediations on the possibilities of life and desire which is a common trope in her later works too. The voice in these verses probe into contradictory impulses: "the desire for adventure and anchorage; expansion and containment; vulnerability and strength; freedom and belonging; withdrawal and engagement; an approach to language as exciting resource and desperate refuge" (*Where I Live: New & Selected Poems*).

Another Country: An Anthology of Post-Independence Indian Poetry in English (2013) is a Sahitya Akademi anthology on contemporary Indian poetry in English edited by the poet. The compilation is an attempt to shape an interest in readers for poetry in every language. "It is equally clear that in their most interesting works, these poets are not trying to be Indians or contemporary or cutting-edge or postcolonial in any trite or self-conscious way" (*Anthology of Post-independence Indian poetry in English*). *When God is a Traveller* (2014) won the Sahitya Akademi Award for English in 2020. The book is a religious collection of poems in the formula of Bhakti tradition that was a counter-cultural movement in spirituality. 'How some Hindus Find Their Personal Gods' is an exemplary poem in this book that highlights the personal side of one's religious beliefs. Arundhathi Subramaniam does this by representing the God, 'Karthikeya' we try to seek not as a deity in the temple but as a traveller or spiritual vagabond who explores the whole world to realise his own self. The book has been shortlisted for the T.S.Eliot Prize, awarded the International Piero Bigongiari Prize in Italy (2015) and was also the Season Choice of the Poetry Book Society.

Eating God: A Book of Bhakti Poetry (2014) is an anthology of sacred poetry inviting readers to revisit the Bhakti tradition by bringing in songs of mystic poets like Kabir, Mirabai, Nammalavar, Tukaram, Akka Mahadevi, Chandidas. It mainly features classic translations of poems by A.K. Ramanujan, Dilip Chitre, A.K.Mehrotra, Jerry Pinto from various bhakti movements in India from the eighth century to the eighteenth century along with newly published ones. Another anthology, *A una poesia non acora nata* (2018) was published in Italy under the publishing house Interno Poesia which was translated and edited by Andrea Sirotti. *Love Without a Story* (2019) is a beautiful collection that provides the readers with insights into moments of daily life in a very subtle and meditative manner. Besides being a remarkable collection of love poetry the poem muses upon theme like integrity and mortality along with strong revelations about one's internal world, a child's observation of its outer world, about men, identity, nostalgia, voices of women and similar themes that displays the coming of age of Arundhathi Subramaniam as a poet.

Besides being a columnist on culture and literature for *Time Out, Mumbai*, *The Indian Express* and *New Woman*, Subramaniam writes on dance and literature as an arts critic in various journals including *The Times of India*, *The Hindu* and *The Indian Express*. Her works have appeared in anthologies like "A Decade of Poetry" in *Poiesis: A Journal of Poetry Circle* (1997-98), *A New Book of Indian Poems in English* (2000), *The Dance of the Peacock: An Anthology of English Poetry from India* (2013) featuring 151 Indian English poets and *Travelogue: The Grand Indian Express* (2018). Translations of her works are available in Hindi, Tamil, Italian, German, and Spanish. The author has been invited to many literary conferences in different parts of the world including UK, Italy, West Africa, Israel, China, Turkey, Spain, Holland as well as in various parts of India, Nepal and Bangladesh.

Prose Works and Accolades Received

A well-known prose writer on Indian spirituality, she has also written extensively on culture apart from being a long-standing arts critic, anthologist, poetry editor and performing arts and cultural curator. As a prose writer, her books include *The Book of Buddha*, published in 2005 which was a bestselling biography of a contemporary mystic. Her deep understanding of Buddhist philosophy along with her spiritual inclination has resulted in a very sensitive and passionate portrayal of Gautama Buddha. A truly democratic belief held out by Buddhism is that it holds out the opportunity of self-realisation for all. This is what interests the author the most. The author explores the enduring impact Buddha has among questors even today.

Sadhguru: More Than a Life (2010) is a biography of her spiritual guide, Sadhguru Jaggi Vasudev, a young agnostic who turns into a spiritual Guru after his experience of enlightenment. This is based on Subramaniam's talks with Sadhguru and his speeches on various occasions and archival material from the Isha Yoga Centre in Coimbatore. The book is a reminder that in order to realise oneself there is no need of religious sectarianism, piety or holiness. *Pilgrim's India; An Anthology* (2011) is a collection of essays and poems on sacred journey taken from *The Katha Upanishad* as well as Fa-Hien, Basavanna and Kabir to Paul Brunto, Richard Lonnoy, Amit Chaudhuri, Arun Kolatkar and others who have undertook pilgrim trails around India. *A Lovely Strangeness* is an essay on poetry published in the *Outlook* magazine in 2014. *Adiyogi: The Source of Yoga* co-authored with Sadhguru in the year 2017 is a tribute to Shiva, the Adiyogi; the forebearer of mysticism. *Women Who Wear Only Themselves: Conversations with Four Travellers on Sacred Journeys* (2021) is her real-life encounter with four self-contained female spiritual travelers in the South of India.

Throughout her literary career, many awards have been bestowed on Subramaniam. Apart from the Sahitya Akademi Award and Piero Bigongiari Prize mentioned above, she has also received Trinity Arts Festival's Lifetime Achievement Award, Raza Award for Poetry, first Zee Media Indian Women's Award for Literature (2016), first Mystic Kallinga Literary Award (2017) for her work in English Literature, the Charles Wallace Fellowship, Visiting Arts and Homi Bhabha Fellowships. *When God is a Traveller* bagged the inaugural Khushwant Singh Memorial Prize for Poetry which was announced as a part of ZEE Jaipur Literature Festival.

Female Mystic Voice in Literature

Arundhathi Subramaniam is known as the pioneer of Bhakti poetry in modern India. In 1997, the author had gone through a life changing experience that turned her focus from philosophy and literature to mysticism. She describes it as plunging into a world of wordlessness and emptiness where everything seemed unreal and filled her with terror; a kind of experience that only mystics had before. To understand this experience, she started devouring mystics like Saint John of the Cross, Rumi, Meister Eckhart, Ramakrishna, Ramana Maharishi in desperation. The quest longed for seven years that took a turn when she ended up finding Sadhguru at a talk in May 2004. This spiritual journey was like a process of unraveling her inner space that underwent different phases of fear, doubt, impasse and peeling the self that finally made her a committed seeker. Now she is a disciple of the Indian Yoga teacher and author, Sadhguru in his organisation Isha Yoga Centre in Coimbatore.

Through her spiritual journey she has come across mystic poets whose voices began to fascinate and intrigue the poet. Their voices are anti-status quoist, dangerous, passionate and even unabashedly erotic often. In these voices, we find no binaries like the material and the spiritual, the earthy and the existential or the flesh and the spirit but everything appears as a part of a seamless continuum. The female voice enjoys much freedom with the Divine. Subramaniam was thus inspired to explore voices of Meerabai, Lal Ded, Mukta Bai, Andal, Janabai, Akka Mahadevi, Soyarabai and those ranging from Kabir and Shah Latif to Salabega and Annamacharya in the literary festivals she curated.

As a poet when the mythological and modern are intermixed in her poetry, she gets a greater satisfaction of laying outside something deeper within her and it makes the narrative linked to a wider expanse of life. The allusion to mythological characters is a way out to heal the author and bring in a more powerful expression that appeals to a collective human consciousness. This spiritual enquiry was about a move towards intense and heightened aliveness for the author. The mystic voices helped her to realise that intimacy and spaciousness, love and freedom are mutually existent. Therefore, from the more contemplative traditions of Buddhism and Advaitam she was drawn to the Bhakti marga of the mystic poets in her journey of spiritual quest. While her earlier work *The Book of Buddha* portrayed an unlicensed questor who went from riches to rag, her later works *When God is a Traveller* and *Eating God* touch upon the licensed relationship with the Divine and delirium of Bhakti tradition.

Elements of Performance in Poetry

Arundhathi Subramaniam belongs to the vast heritage of Bombay poets. The tropical garden of National Centre for the Performing Art situated in Bombay provided a meet-up place for reading out the poets they loved. Reading poetry in public gatherings can be traced back to the custom of reading in coffee houses by Beat Generation poets of America in 1950s. Recent upsurge in literary festivals has added zest to poetry by allowing a platform for poetry to collaborate with other art forms and discourses. Subramaniam presented her views on how to read a poem at the inaugural talk of Navadhisha, a dance conference held in 2019, which focused on the theme "Syntax and Semantics in Indian Classical Dance". Despite the fact that Subramaniam had read poetry at various festivals including Bengaluru Poetry Festival, Ledbury Poetry Festival, Kerala Literature Festival and International Centre Goa, much more recently online platforms like Facebook, YouTube and so on serve as an alternative in the absence of gatherings of this sort. Moreover, Subramaniam has curated several festivals around Bhakti poetry such as 'Stark Raving Mad' at the NCPA in 2014, 'Mystic Kalinga' in Bhubaneswar in

January 2019, 'Wild Women' on women mystics conducted in Godrej Dance Theatre and Experimental Theatre on April 2019 at NCPA.

'Stark Raving Mad' was an attempt to put 'bhava' on stage. Meanwhile, the third edition of Mystic Kalinga Festival aimed at celebrating the formless divine invoked by Bhakti Movement exponents; bringing together dance, poetry, music and discussion by eminent scholars, seekers and artists. The aim was to extract the essence of Bhakti poetry. 'Kalinga Literary Festival – Bhava Samvad' was a webinar series hosted online in July 2020 to regenerate the literary spirit in times of disillusionment and finding out new ways of leading a normal life. 'Wild Women' was a two-day festival of poetry and music dedicated to mystical and female voice. The festival combined the "sensuousness and immediacy of dance and music and the crispness and clarity of the well-chosen spoken word" (Griffin) so that the women mystics who had remained unheard shall be heard, sung, danced and declaimed. The celebration included four major translation projects of sacred poetry, discussions on female body and Bhakti poetry, conversation and folk song, performance of sacred music, Q&A session, talk on female mystic voices, a music covert on women mystics of Maharashtra and Rajasthan and a musical *tour de force*. These festivals reveal the true potentiality of Bhakti poetry or literature to connect today's fragmented society by churning out its performative quality. The principal element that contributes to the performative quality of Bhakti poetry is the personal dialogic discourse the poet has with the self, God and an audience at once. The event Subramaniam has collaborated with the famous dancer Allarmel Valli at NCPA for performing the famous Bhakti poet Annamacharya is an exemplar of the above element. On this account, it can be argued that Arundhathi Subramaniam plays a pivotal role in uniting art and literature thereby breathing life into the latter. Subramaniam can undoubtedly be regarded as a poet who deals with the modern-day human experiences influenced by "the aroma of the private life of the experiencing self" (Nagarajan 6).

Works Cited

"An Anthology of Post-Independence Indian Poetry in English", Sahitya Akademi, 2019, sahitya-akademi.org.in/?product=another-country-an- anthology-of-post-independence-indian-poetry-in-english. Accessed 12 Aug 2021.

Griffin, Peter. "The spiritual path is fierce, greedy and wild'. *The Hindu*, 24 Apr 2019, www.thehindu.com/books/the-spiritual-path-is-fierce-greedy-and-wild/article26933750.ece. Accessed 13 Aug 2021.

Zachariah, Preeti. "Hanging out with verses: with poet Arundhathi Subramaniam". *The Hindu*, 14 Nov 2017, www.thehindu.com/life-and-style/travel/hanging-out-with-verses/article20444106.ece. Accessed 16 Oct 2021.

S. Nagarajan. *Contemporary Indian Poetry in English*. Macmillan, 1977.

"Where I Live: New & Selected Poems". *Bloodaxe Books*, 2021, www.bloodaxebooks.com/ecs/product/where-i-live-new-selected-poems-920. Accessed 11 Aug 2021.

CHAPTER 6

Knots of Umbilical Cord and the Memoir of Dislocations

Sreeshma M.

"It comes from my own experience, mainly. The personal is political like nothing else can be."

Annie Zaidi

The world outside exerts high influence on the inner landscapes of the writer and it blooms the creative thinking. The roots of every individual remain untouched within them despite of the changes that happen to the surroundings of human existence. We tend to observe the changes and these experiences can stir the perceptions to form a unique view. The experience we unearth also creates the political stands. Annie Zaidi makes it clear that each individual is the sum of what they really are and it is depended on the story told to us.

Indian English Literature is the body of works written by Indians in English language not in the native tongue and it voices the culture and analyses the tradition and history of India with a deep sense of nationalistic feelings and brings out the realities capturing each and every emotion. Indian writers are making tremendous contribution since the inception of the genre and have succeeded to strike a blow in the global market with a unique trademark. The writers, be it be poets, novelists, essayist and dramatist have always tried to portray the happenings in the Indian minds and reflect it in the words with all the essence and has also paved way for the discussion of Indian trends and mindset internationally.

Indian English literature has an independent status with the wide range of themes that it deals with reflecting the socio-political structure, Indian culture, traditions and life style. Each of the events happening in and around India, those affecting and not affecting, those that creates ripples and does not create ripples have been the subject matter of creativity of the writers and penned with distinctive style. Along with these reflections of events the writers also pen down their perceptions and thought process that will coherent all the whims and vicissitudes. Indian English Literature has seen a tremendous shift from 20th century. This genre of literature encompasses a multitude of writers from all spheres of life, despite of gender differences and some prominent figures include R. K. Narayan, Raja Rao, Mulk Raj Anand, V.S. Naipaul, Jhumpa Lahiri, Rohinton Mistry, Salman Rushdie, Kiran Desai, Kamala Markandaya, Chithra Bannerjee, Arundhati Roy, Vikram Seth, Ruskin Bond, Aravind Adiga and Amitav Gosh.

As time progressed one can see a sea change on the concerns and themes of the Indian English writers. The stories that centred on Indian independence with high patriotism sprouted in *Rajmohan's Wife* continues the sway with the recent turmoil in the land. The stories of the "sons of soil" are also entangled with the shared nationalistic feeling of the people staying abroad. Thus, Indian English Literature exerts the presence across the globe. The concept of home, identity, diaspora, alienation, identity crisis and dislocation has always been the major theme in the writings as we always looked to redefine our existence connecting ourselves to various surrounding factors. Narratives are often weaved around partition and embeds with the socio-political scenario where existence is threatened and embarks journey of emotional upheaval.

The upsurge of new vision and thoughts have sprouted through numerous authors and made prominent contributions to the genre. Annie Zaidi remains the eloquent symbol representing the current trends of Indian English literature. She as an author has set her writings with a unique insight and persuasive voice. She is a freelance writer, based in Mumbai, who began her career as a reporter in the leading newspapers and magazines like Frontline and Mid-Day. She chooses a distinctive style of writing encompassing various genres. Her first book is a collection of essays titled *Known Turfs: Bantering with Bandits and Other True Tales* was nominated for the Crossword award for non-fiction. The works moves between the style of reportage to travel to memoir and it gives detailed accounts of the realities like the chaos in Chambal, female infanticide and the resurgence of Sufism. She is one of those contemporary writers who has written many short stories, poetry, scripts for plays and two novellas.

She is also a keen observer of society and has also imbibed strong sense of social justice which is often reflected in her works. She has works written on a wide range of themes including identity, expression, cultural and social prejudice addressing the socio-political condition, how industrial townships are formed on the back of dislocations, relationship with land and the struggles that one face with the life in city. Thus, she lets the world know what she thinks and efficiently puts it into words. Her latest work *Prelude to a Riot* won the fiction book of the year 2020 at the Tata Literature Live Awards and was also shortlisted for the JCB Prize for Literature this year. The work is more concerned on the shattering of the body of town, communal disharmony and the focus is less on the fate of individuals. The novel set in an unnamed town of South India is narrated through multifarious voices where each live are intertwined with elements of violence. Thus, she reflects the realities in our homeland.

For her innovative thinking of grounding herself she won the 2019 Nine Dots Prize for the work *Bread, Cement, Cactus: A Memoir of Belonging and Dislocation.* It explains her roots of existence and the social life in the milieu of cultural, political, physical and emotional landscape of her experiences. Her novella *Gulab* is set in the spooky world telling paranormal activity and mystery through deliberate silences and pauses. Her collection of short fiction is titled *Love Stories # 1 to 14.* She also edited the work titled *Unbound: 2000 Years of Indian Women's Writing'.* The work details the writings of women of the past 2000 years leaning with the questions of gender equality and redefining the term women's writing. Her scripts also have wide acclaim and So many Socks has been nominated for META awards and Jam has won the BBC's International Playwriting Competition 2011.

Annie Zaidi submitted an essay titled *Bread, Cement, Cactus: A Memoir of Belonging and Dislocation* as an answer to the question Is there still no place like home, for the Nine Dots Prize, an international competition. She says: Whether it was about my village, or about my relationship with the land itself and where that comes from… or about the industrial township in another context – in my head these were separate books. When I saw the topic, all the ideas started to come together. I was thinking about these as disparate, but the topic forced me to draw connections between them. (Zaidi)

Thus, reveals to us how she was able to weave through the life and conflicts. She was able to pen the concept of home and the notions of belonging in an exuberant manner. She has always felt dislocated and remained with a fractured identity throughout her life. When she saw the question put forth for the Nine Dots Prize everything popped out by means of a quest to prove herself, her identity and existence.

Edward Said opines that "dislocation is a fate with lasting, indeed, grotesque unfair results". Multiple dislocations cause difficulties in identifying oneself as the individual is whirled into various locations and relocations. By piecing together various senses and fragments of experience one defines oneself and connects to the locations. Annie Zaidi has spent her early years in the industrial township of JK Puram in Rajasthan. She defines the place as a set of tasks and norms that can only feed for the living but cannot give a ground to stand firm. She makes it clear that she always fails to answer the question about her place or home and feels she is part of every nook and corner she has been. She associates or describes herself as an intact of the places she has visited. This gives a detailed description of the concept of belonging and dislocation as hauntingly. She is more obsessed with the rural and cosmopolitan regions than the metropole cities which makes her unique as we have many writings and fictions as a tour into urbanity.

The title Bread, Cactus, Cement is associated with the revolving events of her life and the condition of the land. She intermixes the sense of belonging and the sense of dislocations in the work. Cactus is her first memory with the land, bread is suggestive of the condition of her mother and other Indians who moved out of various locations to earn the bread of living and cement is associated with the industrial backdrop of the town. Cement also stands as a symbol of industrialisation in the rural backgrounds. This work brings out the personal experience of the author entangled with the social and political realities of the land. The question of home is a burning sensation in the mind of every individual especially in developing land like India. The concept of home and dislocation has roots in the Indian minds from an early age. We, Indians have faced the partition of the land, dissecting human emotions and beliefs. Annie Zaidi was able to turn each location into memories and recollects her life in various frames.

Her ancestral village was a place where all malicious acts took place and the current living town has high hiatus from it. As she looks back into the city of her birth, that has grown into an industrial township, she is devoid of sense of belongingness. Though we say industrial township as a polish word, colony is what is used to describe such places and the urban residential complex. The life there was of discriminations in the means of the living style and everyone was categorised to elude the feeling of belonging. She defines land not as a piece of field to rest or make a living, instead, it promises a life without fear of being attacked. The emotion attached to the concept of land and the way of looking at it is described to reveal the social segregation and the transformation that happens is associated to every reader.

Each of the essay pinned by her are standalone essays and it is the portrayal of the personal events along with the political condition of the state and redefining the concept of home. She weaves the tales of tribesman of various communities and shows how they are neglected and exploited. The stories of Bhil tribesman who faced the terrible consequences of the tribal dispossession are detailed. Her tales designates the over throwing of the tribal chiefs with an embodying of genealogies and folklores. The tales bring forth the iconic inkling of losing power and losing ground.

The migrants to the towns, the one's shifting between their native place and their work space are often marginalised and they juggle with the belongings and dislocations. She finds and understands the fragility that hovers around such people and tries to fit them into the circle. Tribesmen, rural folks and minorities face subjugation and are left with dilemmas. The concept of home sounds bizarre to them. When Zaidi expresses about a landscape, she brings it alive through the descriptions of the anecdotes and conversations of the natives.

She moves through the life of an Indian crossing various hurdles and differences set forth by the society and defines the concept of home. She also marks how the concept of home alters with the identity as a female in India as it is always associated with the marital ties condemning their right over place of birth. The detailed narrative of marriages and the condition of the daughter in law in the house are pictures of sufferings and female dislocations. She also hovers around the various aspects of Indian social life like the transportation facilities, tastes and the socio-economic changes to redefine home. She weaves her writing reflecting the socio-political condition, partition, religious freedom and the narrowing cultural terms. Her definition of India how she identifies herself.

She also ties the rapport between language and sense of belonging by saying that language politics is knotted into origin politics. The myths and the tradition are described to show the sprouting of discrimination and how food divided people. The concept of feminine dislocations and the plight of women in India in locating their identity and belongingness is pinned in her narrative offering stark realities of the socio-political milieu of Indian society. Throughout her life she has the quest for identity by pinning her choices.

The concept of home and dislocations happening are skinned through the events from all walks of life despite of the urban-rural divide. The association of power with assets like home, and, when power vanishes, the ground also turns to fumes are re-established. She puts forth questions more powerful than the answers. She quotes from *One Hundred Years of Solitude* by Gabriel Garcia Marquez "a person does not belong to a place until someone beloved is buried there". She writes:

> My mother says, wherever you can trace your bloodline, that place is yours. Yours as much as anybody else's. By that measure, the province of Uttar Pradesh is flecked with my blood. Not just Uttar Pradesh, and not just India. Pakistan too. My history is wrapped up with the history of the Indian subcontinent. Mom is Muslim, from the Indian side; Papa was Punjabi Hindu from the Pakistani side (Zaidi).

These have enabled her to see the dispossession that her mother faced and the chaos that happened to the secular democratic land. She expresses the dislocation she felt and the anxiety of her fractured identity and ends the narrative posing powerful questions and evokes a counter solution of home. These are deliberate ways of expressing the dislocations and the growth of industrial townships in the land that created a cluster of people.

Annie Zaidi cannot really pin her identity into one geographic location as she firmly deems that her identity is weaved from all the locations she has gone before. She finds home as a sweet place where she wants to return always and has also thought it as morning mist. When the entire world revolves dynamically home remains a constant icon despite of the notions of dislocations. Home stands equally for all diversions and instabilities alongside giving a firm grip to the roots. Whether there is transformation in the rural setting to the industrial townships or any other dislocations the roots remain intact in the depths firming to the heritage claiming the identity. The definition of home and the attempts to evade the dislocations has to be done by the individual mind set. She ends on a beautiful note:

> This too is a way to define home — as that which we have lived and that which will not leave us: the love that will not quit on us, our social habits, our sources of self-esteem, hunger, shame, genes, fragments of solidarity, refuge, and undisturbed rest (Zaidi 143).

India is the land of diversity with strong unifying bonds. We define ourselves by various means of identity to locate the existence. Annie Zaidi sets the high flames of every reader by bringing concepts and reflections that are close to one's existence and plays a pivotal role in forming perceptions. Her notions of identity and belonging is rooted in her land and she also expresses her sorrows of its impossibility. By uprooting various micro stories from her life, she fills up the gaps as she excavates the excluded and silenced from the dominant main stream society. She pens down in the most unique style of narration often intermixing various genres of writing. She stands clear in her objective and strike the thoughts directly to the reader after forming straight perceptions. Home reflects significant events in one's life and nostalgically reflect personal histories, liminal experience and the psychological intricacies. She as an author of eminent themes can ignite the thoughts that every layman in the country and across the globe can relate.

Works Cited

Said, Edward. Orientalism: *Western Conceptions of the Orient*. Penguin, 1985.

Zaidi, Annie. *Bread, Cactus, Cement: A Memoir of Belonging and Dislocations*. Cambridge University Press, 2020, Google.

Zaidi, Annie. Wikipedia, Wikimedia Foundation, www.wikipedia.com. Accessed on 21 July 2021.

Zaidi, Annie. "Interview: Annie Zaidi on the Nine Dots Prize and chasing 'The call of blood'. Interview by Riddhi Dastidar. The Wire, 30 May 2019. thewire.in/article/culture/annie-zaidi-nine-dots-prize/amp. Accessed on 23 July 2021.

Zaidi, Annie. *Prelude to a riot: A Novel.* Aleph Book Company, 2019.

Zaidi, Annie. "Women always find a way of telling their stories". Interview by Kiran Manral. Shethepeopletv, 30 May 2019.

www.shethepeople.tv/news/author-annie-zaidi-interview-nine-dots-prize/. Accessed on 25 July 2021.

CHAPTER 7

Babitha Justin: Scars, Illness and Surgeries – A Women is Claiming her Body Back

Arsha S Pillai

Twentieth century has witnessed the dynamics and versatility of Indian English literature in its letter and spirit. It completely drifted away from the cliched topics and started to unravel the dilemmas, identity crisis, helplessness and emotional conflicts into the spotlight. Reading about city or sexuality, missing or identity; the roots run deep into the conflicted and destroyed Indian psyche. Poems with an intensified vigour start to address the problems of the present and the past that constitute the rebellion of confused Indian spirits. Writings of tribes and voices of the marginalised can be heard. Every writer is linked to each other at core by the enticing Indian myths. The world of chaotic realities found peace in the pre-existing myths, peace mantras and spirituality. Women writings are sharp-tongued causing piercing effect that they often wound the reader with a sharp smile. Religious and spiritual enquiries are reflected in many works. Performance poetry and discussion through online and offline gatherings make Indian poetry more appealing and outgoing genre.

Body trauma and post-traumatic stress in the post-operative period, often portraying women to the core is a recent trend in Indian writings. The pre-hospital and hospital trauma, its celebration, resistance of mind over body are odious themes that are portrayed by Babitha Justin in her writings. She makes us remember Sylvia Plath in her handling the themes of death, diseases and scars. One must probe into a woman who smiles to all pains and carry a body that buries thousand post-operative scars beneath. She is a woman who stood against all power centers, whether it is religious or gender biased. Her paintings need a peculiar attention while reading her as an artist. *Nude Series of Men*, *Yakshi* and other paintings are like poetry or they contribute to each other. The autobiographical touch and personal comments make these poems more realistic and vulnerable. The reference of scars, lipsticks shades, hospital beds make her poems a true celebration shedding prismatic colours in light.

Babitha Justin is a painter, writer and academician. Her paintings are sold across globe and have an international audience. '*Of fireflies guns and the hills*' (2016) and '*I cook my own feast*' (2019) are her poetry collections. Her poems discuss religious discomfort as in the '*Church Goings*' and racism in '*An Anthem for Brown*'. Alumnae of University of Hyderabad and Jawaharlal Nehru Vishvavidyalaya, she is currently teaching at Indian Institute of Space Science and Technology. One of her short stories, '*Yuppie Diary: A Night in Godawari Hostel*' is a part of MA syllabus in Tanjavur. Her paintings like *Maramkeri Maria, Gypsy Singer, The Pator of Nartiang, Fisherman at Vellayani* and *Buddhist Boys* allures the heart of the viewer. As a woman who has undergone many surgeries and carries a scar upon her face, she looks into herself as a source of light. Her poems are a celebration of the visibility of scars in women; both mental and physical. The painting brushes and the surgical scissors merge into one and she experiences the artistic joy. Apart from other writings, the author intends to study the themes of surgeries and body politics in particular.

From '*Monday to Sunday*', '*Twice Born*', '*Rain Therapy*' and '*Before Therapy*' are some poems that analyse a post-operative mind rather than body. An incised feminine mind is analysed through a poetical framework. Babitha Justin raises the question of what happens to a mind after a significant surgery that alters the raving beauty conceptualisation. A surgery that saves the physical health distorts the inner peace is obscurantism. To restore or reclaim herself she applies crimson lipstick in her lips while leaving the hospital premises. It is flabbergasting that isolate places like hospital beds become places for flirting. Babitha's poems are the need of the hour that it raises as emergent art that explicitly presents the departure of subculture from the existing pattern of trauma writings.

Indian English Literature gave taut prominence over traumas in hospital writings, but heroines caulked it with real thoughts on academics versus home and body versus sex in the surgical bed. Her autobiographical touch gives new lights on educated working class women. Each time she feels joyous, de-stressed and a biblical resurrection. Like John Donne who wrote metaphysical poems and holy sonnets, Babitha's poems show a combination of both. The narrator celebrates the mind and body in her works that seems to be in conflict with each other to have both. Babitha portrays women body that repeatedly undergoes incision. Wounded body in excruciating pain and scars made of surgical cuts made it possible to write poetry.

She adopted a different style of writing, experimental poems bold enough to establish Indian ecriture feminine as an intentional attempt. She contemplated over themes of death, pain, and women roles in a joint family. The question of life she aspired for and her responsibilities blended in her works. She attempts to find a truly feministic mind irrespective of all the shackles, even her own body. She is bold enough to speak about a sexual desire she feels to a doctor during the surgery. Her unconscious feminine self is evident in her textual consciousness.

From *'Monday to Sunday'* is structured into seven parts. It is a poetic prose which is set in a hospital that captures a surgical week from the life of a woman. *Thinkil, Chouva, Budhan, Vazham, Velli, Shani* and *Njayar* are the subheadings. The trajectory of a woman's journey from malady to miracle is existent in her jot downs. The name of days in a week corresponds to planets which are believed to have an influence upon human beings. The horoscopic attributes of each day hubbubs the hospital experience.

"Her thighs heaved their magmas of hate into their cellulite folds"-gave a grand opening for the poem. The authoress is happy to have the surgery, to get rid of the lesion which grew into a miniature citrus fruit. The young doctor who fingers into the lesion with a sexual tension is a shocking image to Indian consciousness. The comparison of a cyst to a citrus fruit is often a reference to biblical themes though it has implicit sexual overtones. The authoress found relief in removing it. The reference to heartbeat that gives two possible inferences is also quite interesting. Either she is ill or she is a yogi. But her mind acts superior to body and proclaims herself as a yogini. The writer becomes more of mind rather than body that questions the body undergone the surgical incisions. It's her mind that is undergoing a period of self-reflection about self and purgation. The poems of Babitha Justin carry different layers of meaning in new environments than we experienced till now.

The transcendence of women above maladies into saints amidst of insecurities is all about women who denounce the barriers of her body, at the same time celebrating it. The crimson lipstick and golden glow foundation is an ambivalence belonging to the possibilities. Medical genres and words are jammed in the poems. The last phrase of every section taken from Aramaic language from Kandisa song lyrics elevates poetic sphere.

'Twice Born' is a poem that is very appealing and carries deep layers of biblical connotations. The title of the poem is itself a reference to Jesus Christ.

> A kind nurse comes
> with a cathartic enema kit;
> before each surgery
> I feel like Gandhi.

"Anesthesia takes off its opium wings" is a poetic expression that describes the psychological feelings of the author, often in a trajectory from the peaceful starting from tranquility like Gandhi to trance stirred by opium in the wings of relaxation.

She slowly begins to rejoice in the crucifixion. The poem *'Twice Born'* carries an imperceptible picture of a Christian women in a surgical table physically suffering because of illness. She is attaining a parallel with Christ who is in the cross. The question of wounds is quite engrossing. One is for the mankind and the latter is for a woman mind. Both are crucified and resurrected. The protagonist is not caring about her body or the possible deformations. She is talking to doctors like the Christ talked to thieves.

'Twice Born' progresses through interactions and comments of the anesthetist. He is a means to relieve the pain, both mentally and physically. The persistence of the crimson lipstick in her lips shows the way the women carried themselves. It is the colour that indicates the excess of desires, dreams, paintings and poetry she had, often autobiographical in tone. It can also be a survival attempt of body over mind, struggling in a surgical bed.

> I may fall in love with him
> during the limen.!

Death can be a possible candidate for this man. A woman can even fall in love with death, if it cared about the persisting lipstick and asked about her children that life never had time to enquire about. Her mind would have wished to get free rather than returning to a body that is wounded and subjective to responsibilites. So she can be assumed to be standing in between life and death. The next stanza is all about a surgical bed which reflects the mannerisms of a death bed.

The presence of death makes her poem serrated and vulnerable. Women body in uncomfortable places, recurring hospital lives, surgeries are her favourite themes, ofcourse with which Indain English Literature is not so familiar. She never considers the body as a burden or the surgical pains life taking. Instead we can see a habitually repairing women body and celebration of scars. Each scar is an autograph of blight on life. Body thus becomes a medium of expression of the past traumas. A women in surgical bed carries all the attraction of a feminine body yet the society tend to normalise it as mere a surgical body. Babitha brilliantly breaks this constructed neutrality. Her women characters flirt with the doctors. She breaks the shell of a neurtalised feminity. A woman is claiming her body back.

After surgery, she witnesses herself laid out in the surgical table. The plot widens when she compares herself as a featherweight Ariel gazing down the Scissor happy surgeon (a phrase of paradoxical importance) and my own morphined Caliban. Her mind is separated from the body and looks downwards like an angel of good spirit. Morphined Caliban is again her body itself, Caliban the native, primitive and colonised one is lying in the surgical table. Reclaiming her woman body, that will never be freed from the pain, desires and constructs is more evident. The poem ends when she sinks down from the heights of flying and felt pain once again as a marking that she is alive. She had reclaimed her body, but with pain and scar.

The poems of Babitha Justin stands out in contemporary Indian English writings. The autobiographical depth of her writings attracts the reader and pulls them into the Bermuda triangle of a confused woman's mind. True Indian spirit, colors and absences in her professional life, the inquisitee mind of an artist seeking perfection, the twin artistic intelligence of a poet and painter fills her poetry with a mystic aura.

CHAPTER 8

Visualising Holy Eroticism: A Narrative Glimpse through Sharanya Manivannan

Divya Suresh

With the growing impact of technology in our lives, there is large room for science fiction and fantasy fiction in India. Pulp fiction, characterised by fantasy, science fiction, military, suspense and thriller has a market of its own. Another new genre which has gained prominence is that of novels in digital form or hypertexts. Revolutions in the internet have played an unparalleled role in the birth of these technology-based texts. Along with the mode of writing and publication, the readers' space has witnessed a significant change as books are available to be read in digital formats such as PDF files and on devices like the Kindle.

The revival of an interest in myth and legend is one salient feature of 21st century Indian novels. Myths are the most enchanting form of storytelling. They serve to document past events, explain the unexplainable and act as manuals for morality. Another trend is the remarkable role of the writers in the theorisation of Indian feminism with its distinct focus on the marginalisation, subordination, and empowerment of women from different sections of India. The novels written during the last twenty years meticulously contextualise gender related issues keeping in view the Indian scenario. Women authors and activists have made notable efforts to redefine the identity and position of women besides addressing their pain, aspirations, sufferings, challenges and marginalisation. Traditional misogynistic values have been critically interrogated and marriage and other social constructs have come in for searing scrutiny.

Concern for the differently abled is another important feature of contemporary Indian writing. This concern gave birth to a new area of literary and cultural study called Disability Studies. This branch of critical inquiry takes into account previously ignored subjects related to physical or mental impairment.

There are many contemporary writers who are true to recent trends in writing. They are Meena Kandaswamy, Akhil Katyal, Sharanya Manivannan, Rochelle Potkar, Kavita Kane and many more.

About The Author

As an upcoming writer and illustrator, Sharanya Manivannan, Indian by birth and raised in Sri Lanka and Southeast Asia, writes across a wide range of topics and skillfully weaves fact, fable, and fiction to create strikingly original works. She is sensuous, spiritual, delicate and dangerous in her works. Her poetry apprises her prose and her aspirations guide her ideas. Her major books include *Ammuchi Puchi*, *Mermaids in the Moonlight*, *The Queen of Jasmine Country*, *The Altar of the Only World*, *The High Priestess Never Marries*, and *Witchcraft*. Sharanaya Manivannan is currently writing a personal weekly column, 'The Venus Flytrap' for *The New Indian Express.*

Areeb Ahmad, Co-Editor-In-Chief of the journal *Medley*, opines that Sharanya Manivannan's poems and prose are "deeply human in their fallibility and rife with contradictions, mirror the complexity of our modern lives". Her language is sensual and sublime, brimming with love and longing, fervent in its need to break free from mundane conventions. Mythology holds a central place in her narratives. She merges the ordinary with the extraordinary and the personal with the universal, moulding a new vision. Her works usually feature women who are remorseless and outspoken. She is wise in communicating the untold powerfully in matters of love, longing, desire and heartbreak. *Witchcraft* (2008) is her first full length book. It is a collection of poems and has a foreword by the Peterson Prize winning poet, Indran Amrithanayagam. *The High Priestess Never Marries* (2016) is her first work of fiction. It is a collection of short stories that feature women who seem suspended between relationships, desire and despair. *Ammuchi Puchi* (2016) is her first picture book and the illustrations are done by the Argentinian illustrator Nerina Canzi. This is a poignant story about bereavement and healing where we witness a strong bond between a grandmother and her grandchildren. *The Altar of the Only World* (2017) is a collection of poetry filled with hallucinatory visions, exquisite imagery, raw passions and deep emotions. *The Queen of Jasmine Country*

(2018) is her fifth book and first ever novel based on the recreation of the ninth century Tamil society in poetic prose. The plot revolves around a girl named Kodhai. This is a reimagined biographical story of the Tamil mystic poet Andal. *Mermaids in the Moonlight* (2021) is a beautiful graphic book that enchants young readers. This is the writer's debut work as an illustrator. This book showcases the essence of mythologies and folklore with respect and honour to the culture they originate from. The story is about a mother telling folktales to her daughter Nila about the variety of mermaids residing underwater.

Sharanya's women portrayals delve deep into the female psyche and we find ourselves in their fragments.

Holy Eroticism in The Queen of Jasmine Country

Spiritual Eroticism or erotic representations of the Divine, occupy a pivotal place in religious myths, poetry, liturgy and theology. *The Queen of Jasmine Country* is a startling work of fiction adorned in strong, indigenous, sensual prose. With the ample use of classical poetry, the writer Sharanya Manivannan imagines the life of the devotional poet Andal, whose majestic amorous verses remain well-loved as well as controversial to this day. Andal was the only woman poet among the twelve Alwars (Tamil Vaishnavaite saints) who recited verses in praise of Lord Vishnu and believed him to be the Supreme Being. P. Lalita Kumari, Telugu poet and writer, popularly known by her pen name Volga talks about Sharanya's work thus, "Myths, dreams, desires, the timeless reality of the body and the soul – in the midst of nature's bounty – that is the essence of *The Queen of Jasmine Country*." Sharanya is well-versed in the rituals of ninth century Madurai and she sketches the practice of Paavai Nonbu which is the central attraction of the novel.

Paavai means 'a girl' and *Nonbu* means 'penance'. It is an old age tradition observed by unmarried girls for getting a husband as they desire. It involves getting up in the early morning between 3am to 6am which is termed as the Brahma Muhurtham, taking a holy bath in the temple river and offering prayers at the temple. There are certain rules to be observed while performing this nonbu such as to avoid indulging in worldly matters, leading an austere life, and most of all keeping the mind completely absorbed in the Lord. These activities are observed during the entire winter month of Margazhi, which starts around 15th of December and ends around mid-January. Stressing the importance of Margazhi, Lord Krishna declares in

Bhagavat Gita thus, "amongst the twelve months, I am the month, Margazhi".

A parallel can be drawn here of a Hindu mystical poet saint of the Bhakthi Movement Mirabai and her undying love for Lord Krishna. Her erotic poems and songs were infused with her immense love for the Lord. She considered him as the husband of her soul. Although she wrote in a way that suggested human love but the relationship is in fact a sprititual one. Another similar aspect of spiritual love can be traced back to the Sufi Movement. Sufism entered in India between eleventh and twelfth centuries. This movement strictly discarded caste system. The Sufi saints seek inner purity and believed that love and devotion are the only means of attaining God. They presumed that God is the beloved. This union between the God and devotee is like the flow of poetry, the trance of music, the whirling of dancers in ecstasy. Rabia al-Basri was a Sufi mystic who lived in the eighth century. She was considered to be the first female Sufi saint. Rabia championed love as a path to the Divine and had no hesitation in declaring her intense love for the God throughout her life.

This novel *The Queen of Jasmine Country* can be called as a fitting homage to Andal who had appeared in a dream to the writer in 2014 and urged her to write her story. As a poet belonging to the ninth century Bhakthi Movement, Andal was elevated to the position of a Goddess. She found a physical and spiritual oneness with Lord Vishnu. Sharanya Manivannan imagines the transformation of a young Kodhai into the Tamil poet-goddess Andal. Andal, as the name suggests, is an epithet meaning 'she who rules' and Kodhai means 'string of flowers'. The plotline of the novel closely follows the books *Thiruppavai* and *Nachiar Tirumoli* which are ancient sacred hymns attributed to Andal.

The novel is set in the ninth century in the village of Puduvai in Madurai. In the season of mid-summer rain, a baby was found in the Tulsi grove near the house of a Brahmin garland weaver named Vishnuchittan. The man and his wife adopted this child and named her Kodhai. The author tries to strip Andal of her divinity and presents Kodhai as the daughter of an Alwar named Vishnuchittan. He had a daily ritual of weaving garlands for Lord Vishnu who resides in the Vatapatrasayi temple in Srivilluputhur, Tamil Nadu. Back then women were not allowed to read or write scriptures but Kodhai's inclination towards reading and writing moved her father.

So he taught her hymns, myths and verses. Gradually, Kodhai's affection towards the deity grew passionately. Following her puberty, her fervour for the Lord increased to an extent that she realised her yearning to be His bride. Her conviction of her endless love is astounding in pure depth. Encouraged by her older cowherd friend, Matatilli, teenager Kodhai embarks on a period of penance which is the *Paavainombu* to attain the love she longs for. During this period, she pens down her innate desire and passionate love in the voice of a cowherd woman. These verses are compiled as *Thiruppavai*, the verses of which are still recited in the month of Margali. Desperate to witness her love, she rants at the Lord and implores him for unification, a desire that animates another text *Nachiar Tirumoli*, a darker erotic composition where she invites the deity to be her love. After knowing his daughter's desire, Vishnuchittan thought it was impossible for a mortal being to tie the knot with the Lord. But multiple visions of the Lord in his dreams indicated to Vishnuchittan that Kodhai is the Lord's consort, Nappinai or Radha. Kodhai attained her divinity through her marriage to Lord Vishnu and was later hailed as Andal.

Each night, something that can neither be quenched nor extinguished scorches me from within. It is more than the pleasure my body seeks, the pleasure my hands fulfil in the absence of a lover. Life is at once material and illusory. The merging of the individual consciousness with the super consciousness is showcased in the novel. The novel candidly explores female desire, devotion and spirituality and also presents how an Indian woman is able to abandon the shackles of a conventional society and seek bliss in devotion and writing. In the midst of this narrative, there are tales of women bound by tradition facing the social evils of caste, oppression and social hierarchies. The novel highlights the admirable rituals practiced in the embrace of wild and relaxing greenery. There are no homes with rooms large enough for the wingspan of a woman like me. The writer depicts the trauma of not fitting into as well as withering away.

The plot revolves around many intangibles like love, desire, devotion along with the beauty of the mundane – the fragrance of the flowers, the delicacy of the milk, the sight of the hues of the village, and the touch of the dampness of the Tulsi grove. The narrative is embellished with visually striking accounts, be it the grasslands, the cowherd women, the majestic parade of elephants, the harvest, or the hefty bulls in the Jallikattu. Sharanya Manivannan presents a charming world of rituals of the ninth century Madurai through Kodhai's eyes.

Work Cited

Khurana, Monika. "Trends in Modern Indian English Novel". Vol. III, Issue 1, 2017. IJARIIE- ISSN (0)- 2395-4396.

Manivannan, Sharanya. *The Queen of Jasmine Country*. Harper Collins Publishers India, 2018.

Nirmal, Arti. *Recasting Indian English Fiction in the Twenty First Century*. An International Peer-Reviewed Open Access Journal. Vol. VI, Issue 4, 2020. ISSN 2349-5189.

CHAPTER 9

Janice Pariat: Tracing War and Women Consciousness

Chandana J. S.

The inevitable relationship between life and literature has been evolving to develop emerging theories and practices that move along with the dynamic perspectives of the society. The issues of gender, culture, race and politics are now actively explored and organised, transcending linguistic and social boundaries. The twentieth century Indian literature has been adorned by the works of the famous trio – Raja Rao, R. K. Narayan and Mulk Raj Anand. The contemporary Indian writers like Anita Desai, Arundhati Roy, Aravind Adiga, from different walks of life aim to challenge political and social issues in a wider sense, by creating spaces for the readers to introspect at every level of comprehension. They delve into global concerns by creating an intercultural reality that shapes platforms for different voices to be heard and addressed. Their works are not limited to addressing the poor and marginalised; rather they focus on the different types of lives and the relationship between various cultures. The development and expression of new themes and issues have rewarded them with many recognitions that proclaim the importance of literature to the world.

One such contemporary Indian writer is Janice Pariat who has been creating waves in the field of fiction and poetry by incorporating several social issues into her works. She was born in the North-Eastern state of India-Assam. She grew up in Meghalaya and completed her undergraduate course in English literature from St. Stephen's College, New Delhi followed by post-graduation from the University of London. Pariat is the founder-editor of an online literary journal – Pyrta (2010). Her articles have been featured in several Indian and International magazines including Time Out Delhi and The Caravan. She currently teaches Creative Writing and History of Art at Ashoka University.

The North Eastern states of India are known for their rich tradition of folklore and cultures, but they are also vulnerable to all social and political transformations. Pariat has stood out as a spokesperson of her land, successfully incorporating all the nuances of Assamese culture and traditions in the works. Her writing style also contains the elements of magical realism that makes it identical to Haruki Murakami's works. The stories are often quoted to be unique and illuminating. Pariat's notable works include Boats on Land: A collection of short stories (2012), The Nine-Chambered Heart (2017) and Seahorse: A novel (2014). Her poems are published in collections such as The Yellow Nib Modern English Poetry by Indians (2011), Kavi Kala: The Visual Poetry Project (2010). The narratives have a different style of characterisation that develops meaningful plots and characters.

Pariat fills her works with lyricism and imagery in all its true sense, to describe the beauty and traditions of North Eastern landscapes. But she never fails to examine and unfold the cruel impact of the social and political events that affected its people. War can be considered to be a recurring theme in her short stories, especially in the debut collection, Boats on Land. It won the Sahitya Akademi Young Writer Award for the English language in 2013 and a Crossword Book Award in the same year. The stories in this collection are mainly set in Shillong, Assam and Cherapunji. These compromised the exploited landscapes and some of the major social changes that transformed the face of Northeast India, especially during the 1850s.

Depiction of War

Pariat believes that stories always make way for better interpretation of history and the world. In Boats on Land, she has reimagined her motherland, its people and intermingled the elements of folklore, history, politics and culture. Most of the stories in the collection are likely to be incidents that Pariat heard from her family and friends. She has incorporated both reality and myths to provide a different viewpoint to readers so that the beautiful and chaotic North Eastern landscape can be reimagined in a broader sense. A large historical background is provided in each story that depicts the struggles and oppression faced by the people. Though the stories portray the period of British rule and the World Wars, Pariat used them just as triggers to develop the psychological motivation of her characters. But the background of wars and oppression helped the stories in depicting the issues of subalternity and marginalisation.

The gnawing aftermath of the war and the way in which it percolates to ordinary lives is poignantly depicted in the short story, Dream of the Golden Mahseer that deals with the retired army man and his disturbed mental state. Most of the short stories in the collection picture characters against different historical settings like colonialism, post colonialism, insurgency, disputes between the indigenous people and the partition of Assam. Within these settings, Pariat depicts emotionally weak and unstable characters who have troubled relationships. Contemporary writers such as Arjun Subramaniam and Srinath Raghavan have also talked about India's participation in the Second World War. These two authors made direct allusions to the terrors of war, its aftermath and the role of the army in their works. Meanwhile, Pariat focused on the idea of reality imbued with a subtle touch of folklore, fantasy and imagination in order to provide a clear picture of her motherland and its people who suffer the consequences of war.

Representation of Women

In the novels of Indian women writers of the post-independence era, there exists a trend that explores the theme of modern woman's struggle to find her own identity and position in the society. This tendency is often found in the works of Janice Pariat and other women writers such as Kamala Markhandaya, Anita Desai, Meena Kandasamy and Nayantara Sehgal. Pariat particularly focuses on the various relationships that women find themselves in and their aspirations of the love that they deserve. Her novel, The Nine-Chambered Heart, portrays the story of a woman from the perspectives of nine different characters in her life. The story is traced through the narration of the people who have loved her and the people she has loved. The book contains nine chapters, each narrated by nine characters. Through the young woman, the readers see different dimensions of love that are illustrated in every sense. She shares meaningful relationships with each character that has a transformative power over her life.

The nine characters reminisce about the love that they have shared with the young woman through several accounts that are vulnerable and beautiful. Here, Pariat presents the young woman as someone who seeks and accepts the warmth of love. Though the theme of love breezes through the novel, the unnamed young woman has been groped, photographed nude without her permission and has been seen as a sexual object of desire by almost all the characters. Throughout the novel, the young woman has been exploited by some while adored by others for her personality. The work can be viewed under a feminist eye to discuss how the young woman has been moulded and exploited under the pretext of love. The theme of women and love has often been found in contemporary works of Indian authors. Women are mostly connected to the feelings of love, longing and fidelity, especially in the Indian contexts. Authors like Sudha Nair and Alisha Rai are known to include love, acceptance and desires of women as the major areas of interest in their works.

An honest treatment of the issue of lesbianism is also presented in Pariat's works, especially in her collection of short stories, Boats on Land. The story, "Secret Corridors" in the collection gives a true portrayal of "the lesbian consciousness of the protagonist" (Goswami 29). It focuses on how her sexuality influences her identity that eventually leads to a strong relationship with another woman. The narrative reassures the theory of lesbian feminist scholars that healthy and emotional relationships can develop between women. Another story in the same collection, Boats on Land, explores the life of a young woman who has discovered her sexual identity which made a profound impact on her mind. Pariat has given a truthful and original representation of lesbian life and their identity crisis.

Queer literature flourished as a separate genre that has a profound impact in the Indian context as well. Writers like Arundhati Roy, Amruta Patil and Manju Kapur have been instrumental in dealing with the issues of homosexuality and lesbian consciousness. The significance of their works lies in the fact that they talk about a highly sensitive and vulnerable theme that needs attention. These writers set out to bring out the hidden realities of the society where people struggle with their sexual behaviours that cross all the social boundaries.

Thus, Pariat delves into the theme of modern women from every dimension in order to give an explicit picture of how women are observed and scrutinised by the society and how their disturbed minds cope with the boundaries set by the constructs of gender. The distinctive style adopted by the writer encompasses the subtle blend of reality, folklore and imagery of the landscape that gives lustre to the narratives. The domain of Indian English literature proves to have no limitations as it has now shifted to addressing global concerns and issues rather than merely adhering to the sentiments of their land. It has made an identity of its own by creating a niche for promising Indian writers like Janice Pariat.

Works Cited

Goswami, Harajit. "Lesbian Consciousness and the Subaltern's Voice: Reading Janice Pariat's *Boats on Land*." *The Criterion: An International Journal in English*, vol. 8, no. 8, 2017, pp. 26-36. *The Criterion*, eISSN 0976-8165.

"Indian English Literature: The Themes Of Modern Women In Indian Literature." *123 Help Me*, 123Helpme.com, 16 July 2019, www.123helpme.com/essay/Indian-English-Literature-The-Themes-Of-Modern-PC6JV4AGDNR.

"Janice Pariat." *People Pill*, Prong Media, 27 Aug 2020, www.peoplepill.com/people/janice-pariat.

KD, Anand. "Recent trends in English Literature in India." *International Journal of Research and Analytical Reviews*, vol. 6, no. 1, 2019, pp. 429z-432z. *IJRAR*, eISSN 2348 –1269.

Narayan, Manjula. "Review: Boats on Land." *Hindustan Times*, HT Media Group, 6 Oct. 2012, www.hindustantimes.com/books/review-boats-on-land/story-aIlPGI2mBwg6QCOPI1tP5L.html.

Sripathi, Apoorva. "Why is love furious, fleeting, and foreign? Ask Janice Pariat's new novel." *Scroll.in*, Scroll Media Incorporation, 24 Dec.2017, www.scroll.in/article/862435/why-is-love-furious-fleeting-and-foreign-ask-janice-pariats-new-novel.

Sudarshan, Aditya. "The tawdry heart of the matter: The Nine-Chambered Heart by Janice Pariat reviewed by Aditya Sudarshan." *The Hindu*, The Hindu Group, 23 Dec. 2017, https://www.thehindu.com/books/the-tawdry-heart-of-the-matter-the-nine-chambered-heart-by-janice-pariat-reviewed-by-aditya-sudarshan/article22145964.ece.

CHAPTER 10

Anees Salim: A Follower of Shadow of Death

Georgeena Rajan

The star authors with their celestial works in the galaxy of Indian English Literature has been fulfilling the aesthetic pleasure of the hungry readers since decades. The aura from these poems, novels, short stories and dramas are experienced not only by the native Indians, but also by the global audience. There are many writers in Indian English Literature who are noted for their charm and uniqueness in themes as well as style of writing. They are acknowledged by a number of awards and accolades all over the world as well. Indian Literature has attained an independent status in the realm of World Literature. Versatile themes emerge within Indian writing in English. Most of these works reflect Indian tradition, social values and even Indian history through the depiction of Indians and their cultural roots.

The theme of death has been illustrated in many Indian English novels, poems and dramas in abundance. These novels demonstrate it with outstanding realism filled in deeply knitted characters and plots, carefully crafted in a traditional Indian set up. The distinctive treatment of death as an abstract element stands remarkably in many of these novels. This article discusses the theme of death and sadness in the works of Anees Salim.

Anees Salim is a Kochi-based Indian author, born in Varkala, a small town in Kerala in 1970. He is a school dropout and is currently the Creative Director of FCB Ulka, a multinational advertising firm. He is a successful orator and critic and famous for his talks at the Literary Festivals. He started his writing as a young boy under the influence of the coastal place in Varkala in Thiruvananthapuram. *The Vicks Mango Tree* (2012) was his first published book. This was followed by *Tales from A Vending Machine* and *Vanity Bagh* in 2013. It was his third book that helped him to establish his career as a writer. *The Blind Lady's Descendants* published in 2014 won the Sahithya Academy Award for English category in 2018. *The Small-Town Sea* was his fifth book published in 2017.

He is among the finest living writers in Indian English Literature presently. Anees bagged the Hindu Literary Prize for Best Fiction 2013 for his *Vanity Bagh*, The Raymond Crossword Book Award for *The Blind Lady's Descendants* in 2014. He had also won the Atta Galatta Bangalore Literary Festival Book Prize for Best Fiction in 2017, for his work *The Small Town Sea.*

The Vicks Mango Tree is a book that tells the story of India under Emergency. The story is about the fictional town Mangobaag and the bunch of ordinary people living there. The author's insight into the way ordinary people think and behave comes across one character analyses the other, finds ways to fulfil his or her dreams, makes sense on the world round and get on with the routine. *Tales From a Vending Machine* is the story of Haseena Mansoor, a young Muslim girl employed in an airport vending machine and her string of adventures. *Vanity Bagh*, meanwhile, sketches the picture of a tiny Pakistan inside a big Indian city, against the backdrop of a serial bomb blast. The book is about the life of a boy from a minority community and about hopelessness. More than any other controversies, it is also about distress and religious intolerance. *The Blind Lady's Descendants* is written as the suicide note of a young Muslim from a little known Indian town. He used Varkala, his hometown as the backdrop of this family saga.

Shadow of Death in *The Small-Town Sea*

The Small-Town Sea, the fifth novel is a portrait of a family haunted by death. With reminiscences from his own childhood days in Kerala's Vakala, the novel is something of a homecoming for Salim. The story can be read as an allegory for life that every aspiring artist may experience, combining beauty and steadfastness with mystery and destruction. As the title suggests, the story is set in the landscape of an unnamed sea and an unnamed small town. The sea was "almost a living thing; restless, sleepless and famous for its mood swings". At the heart of this story, is a young thirteen year old boy, on the throes of adolescence and a family crisis. His father, a reputed award winning author, is dying of cancer. The boy and his family spend their livelihood in a city where his father used to work as an advertising agent. The city is presented where tracks for new metro railway service were being laid down. But the family of four – the boy his parents, 'Vappa', 'Umma' and the infant sister called 'Little', relocate to the seaside hometown, as the father wished to die in the town where he had grown up. They rent a house named Bougainvillea on a sea facing cliff. The boy joined a local school where he befriends an orphan boy named Bilal. The father though attended treatment, died in his hometown as he had desired, and the boy finds himself confronted with newer challenges in his life.

The Small-Town Sea is the story of a family, the unique and strong bond between a father and the son, and the story of two friends from absolutely desperate backgrounds. It also weaves a tapestry of memories and anecdotes which are so personal and intimate that makes the reader wonder how much of it was real. The story is told by the boy in the prologue, in the form of a cover letter addressed to a literary agent based in London who had declined to represent his father. The novel is semi-autobiographical as it tells about Saleem's beach home town Varkala, where he spent most of his lonely childhood. The autobiographical elements come in the child and his father called "Vaapa". Anees breaks the suspense by writing in the last pages, that he borrowed the voice of his son for the child protagonist, who too goes unnamed.

The shadow of death looms large over the entire novel. More or less we understand that death itself is a character hidden under the mysteries and pathos. The sadness is portrayed as beautiful as in a realistic manner. Human existence is a mystery, an unsolved riddle, a journey that begins with birth and ends in death. Hence, birth and death are omnipresent episodes of human life. Death is an integral and inevitable part of life, an ultimate end of the journey through world. Frank and Judith McMahon voice that "we may have seen death, read about death, or even close to death, yet we have never died. Thus we face the ultimate unknown, and the fact that our society refuses to admit that death is a natural process". A sense of insecurity and immorality is a common feeling that is mutually shared generally by all the human beings. The story emphasizes the portrayal of life itself, and hence the theme of death is inevitable from it.

In this novel, the father is never portrayed as an overtly attached family man, but he loved the family in his own ways. The chapter where both the boy and the father visit a secret beach, where the father ask the son to head his life alone, facing all the challenges, is heart touching. The sound of death bells provides the background music for the particular scene. Thus excursions to the beach proves to be hideously wrong at the end.

"You should walk either ahead of me or behind me" he tells the boy. When the boy asks why, the father says, "You should learn to walk alone".

His father passed away and their life changed. His mother was forced to make a decision that altered everyone's life. The innocent boy is left behind in his own pathos and miseries. Loss of people close to one's heart is not easy to deal with. The death of his father and the loss of his mother made the condition of the boy vulnerable. People, who are left behind in that process of separation, learn to cope up and adjust in their own ways. For some people they move on, others grieve while a small fraction of them carry the happy memories about the departed ones. The writer managed to hold these despondent emotions together in the novel.

Childhood here is frequently chained by untimely deaths, departures and bad dreams. When his Vappa slips out to coma, he places his fingers on his lips. The power of death seems to be unavoidable. Comic moments in the book underlie a melancholic overtone. Even his imagination too is an exit route from the depressed and submerged grief. The narrator is also prone to nightmares, both when sleep and awake. When he sees a trail of blood on the floor, he imagines that his mother has bled to death in the bathroom. The reality is knitted around the imagination where both revolve round the central theme of death.

Apart from being a master story teller, Anees Salim's oxymoronic style of narration laced with subdued humour and his amazing objectivity lend his craft uniqueness rarely found in the contemporary crop of Indian writing in English. He does not seem to have a particular target readership for his novels. He simply has transferred his close familiarity and deep insight into the characters of the text in an inimitable style with the stamp of originality. What is most striking of his narration is that the real stories are not present in the lines, but between the lines because every sentence in the novel has longtale to tell about the ambiguity of death and the suffering of life. The struggle for survival is evidently seen throughout the novel. This novel shows that in spite of the inevitability of death, people struggle to live and survive.

Each of Salim's novels has been darker than its predecessor, but *The Small Town Sea* is his darkest yet. All the elements of a black comedy are present in the novel. The terribly ill Vappa on his bed surrounded by relatives planning his obituary while he stubbornly refuses to die, Bilal who invents stories about witnessing pirates battles on seas, the narrator trying to use an injured pigeon in his house for pigeon post etc. add to the elements of black comedy in the novel. While Vappa is stuttering towards his death, the sea keeps fading in and out of the background with each successive moment in the spotlight bringing despair and gloom. The novel captures seemingly innocuous and frivolous instances of one's childhood and serves it as a backdrop to represent how his father's death is also a peripheral act in his life. The vivid imagery prepares the reader for the string of tragedies.

Death as an experience has a different meaning from a child's perspective. Children do not accept the truth of universality of death. When a parent dies, it is obvious that the child craves for the role played by the parent. For them it is not about losing a person, but it is more about losing a lifetime relationship. In this novel, Anees Salim has depicted emotional human relationships and rendered a child's feeling towards the loss of his father and grandmother. Here, the story expresses turmoil of emotions that revolves around death from the perspective of a child.

Death is a recurring theme in almost all his books. In an interview given to The Indian Express, he said that when a person dies, a story is born. He claimed that he uses death only when the story demands it. For him, death is a natural thing to happen in his stories. Apart from death, *The Small Town Sea* also deals with the decay of the body, of a house and of relationships. Anees Salim moves in a unique trajectory in which the autobiographical elements paved the path for expressing many hard realities of Indian life.

Work Cited

Kumar, Praveen. "Literary representations of Death and Affliction in selected contemporary Indian Short Stories". *International Journal of Research and Analytical Reviews.* Vol. 5. No 4. Nov 2008.

McMahon Frank, and Judith Mcmahon. *Psychology: The Hybrid Science.* Chicago: Dorsey Press 1986.

Salim, Anees. *The Small-Town Sea.* Penguin Books, 2017.

Salim, Anees. Interview. Conducted by Anushree Majumdar, 4 May 2017.

CHAPTER 11

Seeking Identity within Obsolescence: A Reading of Vivek Narayanan's Poems

Pravitha Pavithran

Indian English literature is a literary realm that broadly refers to the body of works by writers with an acute and straight Indian descent. It involves the expression of what is known as Indian sensibility and milieu. The beckoning beauty and rich resources of our land attracted the colonisers and wherever they went they took with them not only the tools of trade and colonisation but also their language and literature. The English education campaign in India was spearheaded by the social revolutionaries and the Christian missionaries who implemented the press. Writing in a coloniser imposed language and the growth of Indian English literature serves as a criteria to be categorised under the broader realm of postcolonial literature. The early phase of Indian English literature was characterised by the ideas of intellectual and creative impulse, interest in social reformation and modern education. They mostly dealt with the life of kings, queens and the upper class. The later phase was concerned with the common man experiences and sensibilities. There was a wide spread influential current by the British Romantics. While reading about the history of Indian English literature, one could formulate the fact that the yearly Indian English writers came up with a wide range of storytelling, imitating the Western literary style of writing. The novels and the narrative story telling flourished and well received all over the country irrespective of all other facts. The much overlooked category of Indian English literature was poetry upon which Rabindranath Tagore, Toru Dutt, Sri Aurobindo, Sarojini Naidu and her brother Harindranath Chattopaadhyaay excelled as pioneers. The second phase witnessed a Modernist touch in thematic concern and an urge to experiment with the poetical form. Nissim Ezekiel, Gieve Patel and A. K. Ramanujam falls within the second Modernist phase. Using the modern aspects of British poetry they came up with different platforms to portray the Indian reality. The next generation poets including R. Parthasarathy and Jayanta Mahapatra continued the process and become stable to stand alone with any European counterparts. Later Saleem Peeradina, Renjit Hoskote and their group of poets who wrote about the life in metropolitan cities reflecting political and social awareness.

The gradual but extended growth of Indian English poetry reached its peak during the twenty-first century leaving the thematic boundaries porous enough for the new voices to make their entry. The voices were strong enough to mark their place in the tradition of Indian English poetry and discussed the downtrodden canons of Indian English poetry. Vivek Narayanan is one of the younger generation poets writing in English along with Arundhati Subramaniam, Sudeep Sen and Jeet Thayil. He was born to Tamil speaking upper class parents in Ranchi on 1972. He was raised in Southern Africa, mostly Lusaka, Zambia and did his undergraduate and graduate studies in United States. He did his MA in Cultural Anthropology at Stanford and MFA in creative writing from Boston University. He has taught creative writing at the University of Kwazulu and Center for the Study of Developing Societies (CSDS), New Delhi. His collection of poems include *Universal Beach* (2006), *Life and Times of Mr. S* (2012), and the forthcoming work *After-writing through Valmiki's Ramayana.* Vivek Narayanan also tries his hand in designing and facilitating writing workshops. One of the major features that determine the poetical realm and its surroundings is the element of fiction in his poems.

Vivek Narayanan's first collection of poetry, *Universal Beach* (2006), traces his geographical dislocation of being born in India, growing up in Zambia, going to college in the United States and living in South Africa, before moving back into India. The poems in *Universal Beach* have a relaxed narrative feel when compared to his other poems. A ground level reading of the poems gives the impression of a travelogue and the poet details every precise moment into a collective experience. His second collection, *Life and Times of Mr. S* (2012), is a book-length sequence of poems exploring what is called 'identity' and centres mainly on caste, family, class, tradition, etc. Each poem in the collection traces and explores Mr. S's life, his bond with his family members and the society in which he lives. The very first poem titled 'Waking in the Simultaneous Present' sets the overall mood to the collection. The structure of the poem with different arrangement and order of the sentences throws light upon the confused and dazed everyday living of the protagonist Mr. S, spending his life miserably in a hectic city. Sometimes the description regarding Mr. S's day to day life points to the poem is set in a southern Indian state. With its conventional form and involvement with the cultural and linguistic 'pluriverses', the collection is one of the most challenging books of recent Indian poetry.

Vivek Narayanan's poems have a mesmerising quality with each word weighed in with its unique presence. Moreover his open experimentation in form and structure is worthy of serious discussion. One of the main ideas that he wants to infuse in his readers is that of a confused identity. Throughout the poems of his second collection, he explores identity and what may or may not constitute it; family, speech patterns, a homeland or two, caste, literary heritage, class, gender, desire, food. Using abstract language to describe even a minute thing, Vivek Narayanan was so keen in maintaining a safe distance between fantasy and reality and never disengages from lived experiences.

> "Cement is the realest moat to ring around the future. A castle to call my own. We are rough; cement is rough. We carry what we know in it………..."

The lines taken from poem 'Ode to Cement', where he talks about how cement appear most disgusting thing keeping apart its necessity. By writing an ode to a non-living thing, what he means is to put the thing that is alien but palpable in the world.

Once asked about the thematic concerns of the poems, Vivek Narayanan replied that both Africa and India mean a lot to him and both have acted strongly in the formation of the writer as a person. Two major books that count as reasons behind his venture into poetry are *Indian English Poetry: Anthology* edited by Salim Peeradina and *Poetry from Black Africa* edited by Wole Soyinka. The problem of duality as the thematic centre has no effect upon his poems. He is careful not to let himself be categorised as a 'diasporic' or immigrant writer. Diasporic writers, reflect the effects of trans-cultural and trans-national migration on immigrants, who fall into a sense of displacement and discontinuity in alien countries. The common feature that categorises such diasporic writers is their dual identity.

The identity that is being attached with the native country to which they belong and the counter identity forged in the country to which they move, jostle for mindspace. As a writer, Vivek Narayanan also confronts with this dilemma, the question of identity. The prose piece titled "Mr. S's Native" is a clear cut discussion of identifying with nativity:

> "....... Sir, where is your native? Which is to say, short for native place, which is simply to ask not where you have come from, nor, where you're coming from, but where you
>
> Come from"........
>
> "For tell me, troublesome gods, shall nativity be allied with birth or shall it be carried to its limit in genes one direction and genes the other? And,
>
> does it count if your birth was followed in seconds by a change of scenery? Are you indeed eligible at the razor edge of spoken language?.. ..."

The prose piece is a narrative of mental conflict that the poet himself is being exposed to, as expressed through the protagonist, Mr. S. Geographical boundaries, to an extent, shape one's perspective and foreshadow his personal as well as mental well-being. But as a poet Narayanan suggests the idea of poetics of multiple locations. A person may have multiple locations, but his geographical location need not limit his area of imagination. It is the ability of a person to get absorbed in an environment that can be alien to him, but to still come to a compromise with the surroundings. As the poem suggests, nativity is not something that one gets by mere virtue of birth. For Vivek Narayanan, India is his native land by birth, but he has identified himself as an Indian immigrant in the African continent. In a talk with Souradeep Roy and Uday kanungo for Ashoka University, he said that he is not self-identified as an Indian poet or an African poet but he possesses different traditions within him.

Vivek finds some sort of compromise that one had to come in terms with what one wants to say and the language he uses. As a person, Vivek Narayanan has spent most of his years outside the Indian subcontinent and has spoken English more than any other language. But when the time has come to pen down his ideas and creativity into poems, he no longer seeks the aid of "standard" English. Just like some early Indian English writers, notably Nissim Ezekiel and his own contemporaries, the language used by Vivek Narayanan is English that fixed in the framework of Indian traditions. Through the fixing he never points that English cannot be understood within Indian context; rather had given the idea of an Indian English. Vivek Narayanan had made use of words from languages other than English in his poems, especially Sanskrit words. He once said that it took him years to complete reading the Ramayana and he was lost in its depths. According to him Sanskrit poetry operates with very different assumptions from English poetry. His short poem "Area of Mr. S" is marked with the extreme care taken in the treatment of sensory images. He has successfully combined the visual and olfactory experiences.

"...... Sudden conjurings of
space fried likewise
in recurring Saffola-
or
zigzags of inextinguishable shops and
quickly expandable multicolored goods........ "

Life and Times of Mr. S is noted for the series of six poems titled "His Obsolescence ". These poems have a direct connection with the poet's struggle in writing and are presented by mixing up instances from Mr. S's narrative. All the six poems with the same title show the poet's mind being swirled by struggles. The first poem in the series begins:

"That he might, one day,
Slough off this hokum of him, merge into a purity of form.
That in this emerging the world was still remaindered in the
Texture of its husk"

Poetry in its pure form needs to be encouraged. On the other hand, continuous experimentation will make for the finest poetical forms just like the tests of fire make iron stronger. Vivek Narayanan believes that a large part of poem's potential political power or the power to effect change in society has to do with the fact that it can't be tamed. The power of a poem lies in resisting a single reading and having many things going inside it.

Vivek Narayanan's forthcoming work, *After-writing through Ramayana* is to be a retelling of Valmiki's Ramayana. After two contrasting works, Vivek has turned to the spiritual roots of his ancestors, making space for some mythological ideas. Discussing man in his everyday environment has prompted him to turn to myths and legends and what prompted him with such a shift in thematic concerns needs to be analysed. The analysis would take one into the disintegrating political roots of the country itself. Instead of negotiating with the problem of multiple identity and the ways of expressing poetic heritages, what India needs is going back into its spiritual identity.

Works Cited

Back to the tutor EP.2: Poet Vivek Narayanan in conversation with Souradeep Roy and Uday Kanungo". Youtube, 15 Feb. 2021.

Bhattacharya, Sajalkumar, Lahari, Himadri and Arnab Kumar Sinha eds., *Contemporary Indian English Poetry and Drama: Changing Canons and Responses.* Newcastle-upon-Tyne, UK: Cambridge Scholars Publishing, 2019.

Dominic, K.V. *International Journal on Multicultural Literature.* 2012.

Iyengar, R. Srinivasa. *Indian Contribution to English Literature.* Karnataka Publishing House, 1945.

Narayanan, Vivek. *Life and Times of Mr. S.* HarperCollins, 2020.

Roy Souradeep. "Vivek Narayanan on the Question of the Political in Poetry". Youtube, 06 Aug. 2016, youtu.be/GmzhnOFyBXc.

CHAPTER 12

A Study about Meena Kandasamy

Jyothilakshmi M. K.

The writings of Meena Kandasamy created awareness about the disadvantaged lives occupying the sidelines of society. It could create a visual impact among the readers. She broke the long held silence that can also be considered as a mute submissiveness that perpetuates the atrocities against the so-called powerless section. She represented those who broke away from the narrative of victimhood to assume the rebellious self. She has liberated the Indian women writings along with dalit writings quite remarkable with meticulous effort of breaking it away from the saga of anonymity.

Meena Kandasamy is a poet, fiction writer, translator and activist. She has published two poetry collections; *'Touch'* and *'Ms. Militancy'* and four venerable works – *'The Gypsy Goddess'* (2014), *'When I Hit You Or Portrait of the Artist as Young Wife'*(2017), 'Exquisite Cadavers' (2019) and *'The Orders were to Rape You: Tigresses in the Tamil Elam Struggle'* (2020).

In the poetry collection *'Touch'* (2006), Meena Kandasamy exposed the brutal realities of people in the margins by those who enjoy the glorified status of superior. The act of touching involves physical violence in the form of punishment to a dalit body for touching the possessions of the so-called superior castes; the same touch may be the beatings by a husband or a lustful touch that molests her. Her poetry is against the social evils, rigid caste system and gender inequalities sanctioned by Hindu religious fundamentalism and perpetuated by cultural hegemony in the society.

'Ms. Militancy' (2010) is a poetry collection that is an outburst against the violence against women. The representation of love, marriage and sex as hegemonic power structures made her poetry highly political. She continuously urged to have women who have the

readiness to militate. The poetry collection is named after the revolutionary character Kannaki in the Tamil epic.

Her dynamic debut novel *'The Gypsy Goddess'* throws light on the cruel plight of dalit agricultural labourers who were burned to death in south Indian state of Tamilnadu. The incident quilted in the form of novel discusses the supremacy of caste and oppression of power. The claim for better pay had to face bitter experience of in the Kilvenmeni incident of 1968. Political power is a camouflage against the emotion, that is unethical at times. Writing becomes an art of assemblance.

Her work shortlisted for Women's prize for fiction *'When I Hit You Or Portrait of the Artist as Young Wife'* fuses the political and the domestic and proved successful in soldering the personal and the political aspects of life. She presented the empowered, feministic and outspoken but who didn't herself from violence. She attempted to break the saga of worn-out knots existing in our society. Violence has undergone tremendous flux that it get reflected in novel ways. The problems faced by women runs from nine pages to novels blurring the personal demarcating. A lot of things happen around us, it has happened before and continues to perpetuate. Empowerment alone cannot rehabilitate those survive, it's just a refugee.

Her novella *'Exquisite Cadavers'* is a response against her previous work 'When I Hit You Or Portrait of the Artist as Young Wife' who overheard an autobiographical tone in her work rather than focusing on the lives that matter in the happenings around us. She differentiated the process of writing and the writing, her personal life in the margins and the life of Maya and Karim aligned to the centre. The process of writing was contributed with her interactions, inspirations, anxieties and thoughts while she explicitly presented the couple beautifully with their home, arguments and love, in a far off land like London.

Women with power are more vulnerable as they are dangerous, attempts made to silence them makes their voice stronger. Her work 'The Orders Were to Rape You: Tigresses in the Tamil Eelam Struggle' makes it evident that the powerful women and writing about them can also be vulnerable. She focuses on womanness, tamilness and casteness. It captures the heartbeat of women sent to rehabilitation camps where they are abused and it perpetuates. She made them speak for them as it happens to thousands of women. The woman who was denied choice, who wasn't asked for consent and those who disbelieve in justice are represented in her work. "Women raped as a weapon of war are potent tools for political mobilisation and grandstanding oratory, but in everyday life, they are viewed with derision, suspicion, shame" – makes clear the status of women. She has parted from her fancied image of women with guns crawling towards their enemies in valour. A raped women is considered as someone who has compromised with the moral standards of the society, rather than viewing rape as political causing the emasculation of particular community. Her efforts to record those who survived the camps found form in an essay, with narratives of three Tamil women – the wife of an LTTE fighter, a female combatant from the LTTE, and the author herself. Its second part is a collection of resistance poems by female guerrillas and militants.

The woman who decorated forehead with blood and not vermillion, who didn't wear the mangalsutra but a cyanide capsule are the images of poems unwritten. There are women who embrace weapons and not men, who have the readiness to resist the storm of patriarchy. They will lead an era of vulnerable but empowered women in war against the won-out ideologies and constructs of society.

Poems have the ability to subvert the institutions of caste hierarchy. It helped to demystify the traditional beliefs deep-rooted in the scriptures and mythologies that are in a state of stagnancy. The fissure in writing poetry follows the emergence of saga of new women who has the ability to wage war against the oppressive power structures in the society.

The idea of new woman is dominant in the works of Meena Kandasamy. Women with readiness to wage war against the oppressive structures of the society are represented in the poems of Kandasamy. Women were not allowed to raise voice against the dominant structures of power in the society, the socio-political, religious, legal and cultural institutions. It they attempted to raise voice against the atrocities, they will be provided with the tag of hysterics. What happens to women when they try to militate against the tribulation is matter of major concern. The existing socio-political discourse has overshadowed the pain and suffering of the powerless women who attained the status of the 'aborted', 'raped', 'abused', 'prejudiced', 'defeated' and 'materialised'. Because they still wrestle against the phallocentric society that hides the harsh realities of the contemporary society by homogenising the issues. The destitution and emotional trauma of women who have been abandoned by culture and tradition is unknown, they are still unheard.

The characters of Sita and Shurpanaka in the poems *'Princess-in-Exile'* and *'Traitress'* reflects the extremes of feminine existence. The idea of a pure Sita is demolished and represents a Sita dissatisfied by her husband. The portrayal of Shurpanaka took women ahead. She is said to have been "widowed, forsaken and ordered to exist in erasures." She is represented as a lustful woman who had the courage to woo Ram and Lakshman. Desire is considered as a manly attribute in a society that nullify the choices and desires of women. There is a possibility of resistance and rebellion against the injustices in the society. It is possible to get into a place where you could love anything you choose or you could choose anything you love. For recognising the multiple identities it is important to trace the meanings of what is constituted in history, tradition and culture. There is a camouflaged flow of power that resist to explore the intensity of emotions and bonds among women and their responsibilities.

Hegemony of the dominant gender is held strong over the non-dominant gender. As earlier pointed out if women try to give voice to her rage or her desires through a feministic writing, they are tagged as hysterical. Rather than the sensual human bonds of desire, she has dealt with the hard and fast construction of hegemony that degrades them and their rebellion. In her piece of poetry titled 'Nailed', Kandasamy presents the modern woman detained as they are treated as capability deprived to deal with the socio-political and cultural aspects. This may be due to the fear that she may surpass the menfolk. The society doesn't want women to express their views about them or sensitive to family or community. Because there are limits for women as she is supposed to be careful in her phraseology. Language is irredeemably male-constituted and male dominated not only in vocabulary and syntax, but also the rules, classifications and oppositions.

Kandasamy's raw poetry aims at a discourse that seeks to analyse what needs to be changed. The core theme is an active resistance or a revolutionary activism. The title of her first anthology *'Touch'* reiterates the most inhuman stigmas attached to the people in the lower rung of the society as their very touch being considered polluting. She focused on the biased and hypocritical Hindu Brahmanical system. Kandasamy tried to prove the purity of touch which has been artificially transformed into a taboo when a "touchable" gets touched by the so called untouchable human being, the traditional Indian myth of impurity. Touch is rich in its proficiency in exploring the states of mind and genuine feminine sentiments. But these guidelines of impurity aren't applicable when low caste woman is molested. She is touched, tortured but it becomes an act of insignificance. Kandasamy convoluted the sense of touch in her poetry as act of transcendence and as a part of caste paraphernalia.

The Indian society upheld the old social evil of casteism to gain unwanted advantage over the marginalised section. The marginalised groups of India such as dalits, Adivasis, and nomadic tribes lead dehumanised lives. They have been denied the basic rights by the stratified and rigid caste system. They are not treated equally by those who declare themselves to be the civilised section in the society. There is a gap between the education of dalit students and non-dalit students due to their social location and the financial status of their family. Technology is the process by which humans modify nature to meet their needs and wants. Lack of technological requirement for learning purpose has already taken those prejudiced lives. The necessity of the elite section becomes a luxury to those who struggle to fill the empty stomachs while there are human beings who roam around engaged in menial jobs without even having a roof over their head. They are expected to lead mean life, doing inferior and menial works like sweeping, cleaning working in fields and so on. There is a need for revising the current educational policies that along with elementary education, secondary and higher education also be included.

Meena Kandasamy has presented a subversive Ekalavya who doesn't need the right thumb to pull a trigger or to hurl a bomb. Her re-presentations are against the mythologies and scriptures that validate the evil practices existing in society. Her Shoorpanaka is a woman of desire who had the courage to woo Ram and Laxman while Sita had the courage to walkout and pick a random man rather than to remain a chaste wife. Through her works, she exposed the inequalities embedded in the epics Ramayana and Mahabharata that are considered as sacred texts of Hinduism and are preached about by providing the exploiters with godly status. The evil practices mentioned initially are foregrounded and perpetuated by the mythologies through socio-cultural institutions.

She has used the female body and sexuality to resist the age old assumptions regarding feminity. Helen Cixous made a historical pronouncement in 1974, "Write yourself. Your body must be heard". Women must write about themselves, their sexuality as a process of liberation. As Kandasamy has mentioned her unbridled sexuality is her weapon for social militancy. The same woman who was considered as the living goddess and is supposed to bring fortune in the family of the bridegroom is subjected to harassment, humiliation and cruelty. It shows the cruelty embedded in our social system. Respect for womanhood is on the decline and murders, tortures and suicides are on the rise by the hour. It is not only an offence towards the victim but to the humanity at large.

There are absences within dalit writing and women's writing as Ruth Manorama said "Dalit women are 'Dalits among Dalits' because they are thrice alienated on the basis of caste, class and gender". Gopal Guru has rightly pointed out, "dalit men are using the same mechanism against their women which their higher caste adversaries had used to dominate them". A dalit woman's body becomes the locus of intersection of caste, class and gender. The problems of dalit women have been dealt with utmost sincerity in the poems with reference to the oppressive power structures like marriage, love, family and mainstream feminism. Solidarity of women in Indian society is highly contradictory as it has internal factors like dalit patriarchy, political and literary domination by dalit men. She faces physical torture from the family and humiliation from the upper caste men and women in the society. Thus homogenising the issues faced by dalit women by the mainstream feminists will end up in their ghettoisation. Women have the right to standup against any violation of fundamental rights in her personal and political realm. The women represented by Meena Kandasamy are erotic, desirous and rebellious unlike the tamed and passive women.

Works Cited

Kandasamy, Meena. *Exquisite Cadavers*. Context, 2019.

.... Ms Militancy. *Navayana*, 2010.

.... *The Gypsy Goddess*. Fourth Estate, 2021.

.... *The Orders Were to Rape You: Tigresses in the Tamil Eelam Struggle*. 1st ed., Navayana, 2020.

.... *Touch*. Peacock Books, 2006.

.... *When I Hit You or a Portrait of the Writer as a Young Wife*. Juggernaut, 2018.

CHAPTER 13

Search of Identity and the Effects of Missing in Sumana Roy's Selected Works

Ansan Daniel

Indian English Literature flourished rapidly and has attained an independent and distinctive status in the realm of world literature. The cultural, traditional and linguistic differences of different states paved the way for the development of English literature in India. Many regional works were translated into English which reflected a variety of themes and now the literature continues to reflect Indian culture, tradition, social values and even history through the depiction of life in India and Indians living elsewhere. Over the years Indian English fiction has been successful in giving expression to the Indian experience of the modern predicaments. The early history began with the works of Henry Louis Vivian Derozio, Michael Madhusudan Dutt followed by Rabindranath Tagore and Sri Aurobindo. The growth and popularity of Indian English fiction in the 1930s were vested upon the writers such as R. K. Narayan, Mulk Raj Anand and Raja Rao who contributed greatly to bring literary focus to the social issues. The modern spearheads are Arundhati Roy, Sulman Rushdie and numerous other writers such as Sumana Roy, Annie Zaidi, Arundathi Subramanium and so on who are notable for their Indian way of writing in English and particularly for their audacity in breaking the prevailing silence of the society to different undiscussed – marginalised issues. By bringing the issues such as the illegal superstitious practices, political disparities, westernisation, caste discrimination and humiliations etc. as the core themes of many works and thus to the mainstream literary world these writers played pivotal role in restructuring the society to regain its secular and democratic atmosphere.

Sumana Roy is such a prolific writer and uncompromising poet who got pride of place in the hearts of manifold readers of twenty first century with her distinct narrative skills and wide scholarship over various subjects. Roy works as an associate professor of English and Creative Writings at Ashoka University in Haryana, India. She hails from Siliguri, a city in Darjeeling district of West Bengal, India and throughout her works the characters travel through the streets of the city which attracts the reader's attention. One major work which made her popular in the field of literature is titled as *"How I Became a Tree"* published in 2017, a work of non-fiction, is an exploration of self through comparison to trees. The human development in a fast and furious way is being neglected. Hence, it explores the author's adoration for plants, her inner desire to become a tree. The book takes aspects of humanity – birth and death, love, sex, gender, communication, movement – and the comparison of the growth between humans and trees. Roy also explores portrayal of trees in different artworks, from traditional art to the medium of film, and how it has varied across cultures and history. And this brilliant piece of literature was shortlisted for the 2017 Shakti Bhatt Prize and for the Sahitya Akademi Award 2019 & 2020. Other noteworthy works were published in 2019 which includes *Missing* – a novel; *Out of Syllabus* – a collection of poems; and *My Mother's Lover and other Stories* – a short story collection, also edited the recent anthology of the finest animal stories in Indian literature, *Animalia Indica* (2019). For her notable contributions to the literary world Roy has received recognition in prestigious award as long listed for the Man Asian Literary Prize (2008) for her unpublished novel *Love in the Chicken's Neck*. She is also noted for her monthly column titled "Treelogy" in the *Hindu Business Line* wherein depicts the life of plants in detail. Her works are published in prominent magazines such as Granta, The Caravan, Guernica Himal Southasian, Los Angeles Book Review, The White Review, Journal of South Asian Studies and Journal of Life Writing.

Roy's language is lucid and poetic. The simple and elegant style of writing and the reflection of social problems throughout her works have been widely appreciated.

The works of Roy rejected the typical Indian style of writing fictitious or supernatural themes. She takes plots from the epic books, reframes it with the modern thoughts and each work is considered as a voice of the speechless society particularly pointing out different recent issues such as gang rape, relationships, insecurities etc.

Out of Syllabus is the maiden collection of poetry in Roy's literary career. The title reveals the structure of the book and it is a beautiful collection of thirty-five poems. Though the book has no central theme in common it speaks about various aspects of life; distributed in fifteen sections with the aid of various school subjects starting with Mathematics and continues through Chemistry, Physics, Biology, History, Geography, Art and so on. Each topic is refracted through the lens of some aspect of the broader social world outside the classroom. Many poems such as 'Sadness', 'Lust', 'Every girl is Dinner' etc. depict the trials and tribulations faced by women in this modern society. Even the horrors of the rape of a five-year-old girl in Delhi in 2013 incident is poignantly documented in one of her best poems. "There were bottles inside you, and male snot. A syringe in your hair. A button in your palm."

Missing

Sumana Roy's first novel is a modern retelling of the oldest Hindu epic, the *Ramayana*. It is about an incident happened in the life of a visually impaired poet Nayan Sengupta and his wife Kobita. The narration starts in 2012 when Kobita, a social activist woman travels to Guwahati from Siliguri in search of a missing girl who was molested. Every year the North-east Assam is flooded where the girl is missing and the bitter part is the journalists take photographs and make videos of the incident, but no one tries to rescue her. There is a riot in lower Assam from where Kobita last called her husband.

She also leaves behind some set of instructions to be followed for the carpenter to make a new bed before she comes back. Kabir, the only son of Nayan and Kobita is in England, absorbed in his research about Hill Cart Road, the highway that connects Siliguri to Darjeeling and the eastern Himalayas. The novel portrays the internal struggle in Nayan as he lost his one and only support in his life. The story is structured in the form of conversations and interactions between Nayan and others in the house like carpenter Bimal-da, his granddaughter Tushi, helper Ahmed and driver Shibu. Because of his disability, Nayan has no option but to depend on the carpenter and his family to trace his wife who is missing. The anxiety, fear, depression in the mind of the Nayan is the central plot of the novel. The novel is about seven days in the lives of these people.

Indian traditional epic book the *Ramayana* portrays the missing of Sita, the wife of Rama and the fight against Ravana to rescue her, similarly this novel is about the long await of Nayan for his wife. The novel deals with the theme of waiting, drawing striking parallels with the *Ramayana*, as the epic is par excellence of the theme of waiting. Even the name of the main characters – Nayan which means 'eye or vision' and Kobita literally means 'poetry' expresses the intention of the writer to show their long-lasting love and relationship.

Missing and identity of the women is the central theme of the novel challenging the patriarchal societal dominance and suppression of the women. The basic and fundamental rights of the women were once challenged and suppressed by the male dominated society is being highlighted. Missing literally is not the actual missing of women characters instead it is the missing of the husband for his wife. The novel addresses different issues such as inhumane attitudes, lack of relationships, communal riot etc. which highlights the ability of the writer to bring different issues under one umbrella.

My Mother's Lover and Other Stories

My Mother's Lover and Other Stories published in 2019 is a collection of fourteen stories. The stories mirrored the recent trauma affecting the citizens of the post-independent nation. It is about ordinary people suffering from various kinds of curious ailments and each story reflects the true life experiences of different people living in different situations. The book comprises the story of a woman in Darjeeling desperate for a drop of water; a student fixated on reading a love poem due to the failed relationship of her parents; a poet whose writing is considered as an ailment by her family; an insomniac's experience with sleep therapy; a woman's obsession with getting rid of plastic; a young couple trapped in a student's hostel during the 1971 war; a Nepali student passionate about proving that Nepalis are not stupid; a mother who can no longer differentiate between her heart and her head; a young woman on the verge of suicide; a girl who hides her teeth in a palace garden; a girl who treats literature like astrology; a young lecturer who seeks fame but cannot foresee how it will destroy his life; a singer with a mad harmonium; and two old lovers who are on a secret holiday until one of them finds out.

Interestingly, the book starts with the quote of Roland Barthes:

'I have a disease; I see language.'

Each story is being titled and an appropriate quote of famous English writers highlights the theme of the stories. The stories put forth many social issues like water crisis, depression, mental illness, addiction of social media and many more realistic issues.

Blind Water is a heart wrenching story and is narrated with layered metaphors. The central theme is the scarcity of water in the town of Darjeeling but reflects serious issues such as male dominance, the atrocities faced by the female partners in a relationship etc. The existence of man and the concept of God clashes out.

"She can do without God, She cannot do without water anymore."

Another significant story is *My Mother's Head* which is the titular story written from the daughter's point of view of her mother, a poet who hid her identity throughout her life. It comes as a shock to find her mother to have an emotional support, of love, with a man who the children are not aware of. This shock contrasts the tenderness with which her mother's poem words about the man himself. The grown-up daughter discovers the other side of her mother – a passion as wild as volcano underneath the daily humdrum of the woman they were exposed to.

And the rest of it describes about many problems such as mental traumas and the impact of westernisation. The deep emotions of each character expressed through the stories reflect the modern subaltern problems such as identity crisis, dominance, patriarchal rules, marginalisation and the like.

Roy's contribution as a novelist, poet, short-story writer and essayist shows her ability and courage to shed light upon different inhumane activities and issues in the Indian society which remained concealed and voiceless so far. She exists as the voice of the supressed and oppressed downtrodden. Each and every themes in the works differ in plot but all tied to one knot of the liberation of the woman and equality in identity.

Works Cited

An Introduction to Indian Writing in English. UK Essays. ukessays.com, November 2018. Available online.

<https://www.ukessays.com/essays/english-literature/the-introduction-to-indian-writing-in-english-english-literature-essay.php?vref=1>. Accessed on 09 September 2021.

Wikipedia Contributors. "Sumana Roy." *Wikipedia*, Wikimedia Foundation, 09 August 2021. Available online. Accessed on 24 August 2021.

https://en.wikipedia.org/wiki/Sumana_Roy.

Roy, Sumana. *Missing*. Aleph Book Company, 2018.

Roy, Sumana. *My Mother's Lover and Other Stories*. Bloomsbury India, 2019.

Mukherjee, Anusua. "Review of Sumana Roy's 'My Mother's Lover and Other Stories'". *The Hindu*. 22 June 2020. Accessed on 13 August 2021.

CHAPTER 14

A Cry From the Margin: A Study of the Historical, Feministic and Ecocritical Elements in Hansda Sowvendra Shekhars's Selected Narratives

Aneeshya S. Michael

Indian literature during the period of colonisation and soon after the Independence discussed the suppression that we Indians faced under the colonial masters. As a way of creating awareness among Indians who believe themselves to be inferior to the colonisers, the then writers discussed themes of unity, nationality and patriotism. Later, after the withdrawal of the British government, India again moved back to those days of internal discriminations which were addressed by writers who were the representatives of the suppressed class. When it comes to nationalist leaders, the role of Dr B. R. Ambedkar, the father of Indian Constitution, who was "hailed as modern Manu" after his act of burning certain parts of the *Manusmriti*, the classic Hindu law book that discriminates against the low caste people ("Ambedkar, B. R".) cannot be ignored. *Manusmriti*, widely regarded to be the most important and authoritative book on Hindu law "acknowledges and justifies the caste system as the basis of order and regularity of society". The caste system divides Hindus into four main categories – Brahmins, Kshatriyas, Vaishyas and the Shudras ("What is India's Caste System?") and outside of this Hindu caste system were the achhoots – the Dalits or the untouchables" ("What is India's Caste System?"). The years-long tradition of writings by and about the suppressed and voiceless people includes writers such as Sharankumar Limbale, Mulk Raj Anand, Bama, Meena Kandasamy and so many others. These writers unfolded the lives of pain, sufferings, marginalisation and fear of the lower caste people, or the untouchables. Along with the representation of the lives of the lower caste people, the literature of India started to address the lives of 'indigenous people' or 'original inhabitants', who are called using the term, *Adivasi*, which literally splits into 'Adi' or 'earliest time', and 'vasi' or 'resident of'. The state and discourse in India, however, reject the term "indigenous peoples" as it is considered "divisive, undermining the unity of the Indian nation". The government instead recognises most *Adivasis* under the Constitutional term "Scheduled Tribes" derived from a schedule in the Constitution Order of 1950 ("Issue Brief: Poverty and Social Exclusion in India | Adivasis").

An article titled "Ten voices from Adivasi literature" in *The Caravan* begins with the statement, "People want Adivasi literature, not Adivasi writers" pointing out the fact that most of the works discussing the lives of adivasis were and are still written by Non-Adivasi upper caste writers (Poyam). Like all other literatures, Adivasi literature also began with an oral tradition, right from the beginning of the twentieth century. "Adivasi... communities have created oral archives of their histories and knowledge systems, in the form of songs, stories and mythologies, over generations" (Poyam). As far as Indian literature is concerned, Susheela Samad, an earliest Adivasi writer and the editor of the magazine *Chandni*, Alice Ekka, who is considered to be the first Adivasi woman writer in Hindi, Munshi Mangal Singh Masram, who made the primary attempt to codify Gondi grammar were considered to be the pioneers of Adivasi literary tradition written by writers who are Adivasis. Later, writers like MotiravanKangali, who authored *PaariKupaar Lingo: Gondi Punem Darshan* (1989), Jacinta Kerketta, who wrote *Angor* (2016), Usha Kiran Atram, the writer of *Motyarin* (1993), Ramdayal Munda (*Adivasi Astitva aur Jharkhand Asmitake Sawal* (2002), Anuj Lugun, who teaches at the Central University of South Bihar and the author of *Baagh aur Sugna Munda ki Beti* in 2017 came up with books written in their vernacular languages. These works come under the "first writings by people from their community" (Poyam). The majority of Adivasi communities do not have their own authors, especially who write in English, resulting in a situation in which Adivasi literature confines itself in discussing the lives and problems of a few tribal groups who belong to a certain area. There are only a few works which were written in English and thus got a global audience, "since English as a medium of education still remains the privilege of a few" (Poyam). In addition to that, there is a need for the translation of Adivasi literature into English since there are communities like the Koitur community, with a population of fourteen million people, and writers who wrote in Hindi, Marathi and Telugu, which do not have a single book published in English. There were also writers who wrote in their indigenous languages, such as Gondi, Kurukh, Santhali, Ho and Bhili. (Poyam) In order to preserve the tribal literature and to educate people about it, 'Sahitya Akademi', India's National Academy of Letters, has developed the Project of Indian Literature in Tribal Languages and Oral Traditions" (Shankar).

This chapter deals with the writings of a tribal writer, Hansda Sowvendra Shekhar in the light of his controversial work, *The Adivasi Will Not Dance.* He is a medical practitioner by profession, based in Jharkhand. He belongs to the Santhal community, a tribal group with a population of more than 6 million people in the entire world ("Book Launch: *The Adivasi Will Not Dance* by HansdaSowvendra Shekhar"), who were unknown to the world of literature for a long time. He has written a lot of fictional as well as non-fictional novels, novellas and short stories, including *The Mysterious Ailment of RupiBaskey* (2014), *The Adivasi Will Not Dance* (2015), *My Father's Garden* (2018), and *Sumi Budhi and Sugi* (2020) and two children's books, *Jwala Kumar and the Gift of Fire: Adventures in Champakbagh* (2018), *Who's There?* (2020). He has won the Sahitya Akademi Yuva Puraskar in 2015 for his debut novel, *The Mysterious Ailment of RupiBaskey,* and was shortlisted for the Hindu Prize and the Crossword Award. His *The Adivasi Will Not Dance* brought controversy, and was banned by the government of Jharkhand, claiming that it has presented the Santhal women "in a bad light" (Kumar). He was suspended from job for the same reason (Datta), and released by the High Court of Jharkhand (Kumar). Despite these controversies, this book was also shortlisted for the Hindu Prize. His works were also shortlisted for the JCB prize (*My Father's Garden*), and the Neev Book Award and the Crossword Award for Children's Writing (*Jwala Kumar and the Gift of Fire: Adventures in Champakbagh*). As it has been already mentioned, there are only a very few tribal writers who write in English, and Hansda is one among them from the Santhal Community ("*The Adivasi Will Not Dance* By Hansda Sowvendra Shekhar || Review || Santhal Tribe Stories"). Even though he threwlight on the lives of the Santhals in Jharkhand and thus represents the voice of the unheard voices, he refused to be called as the voice or a representative of the Santhals, claiming that he does not intend to bring any kind of politics in it; he just told the stories he has to tell, and he chose the lives of the Santhals for that is the only thing he knows ("In Conversation with HansdaSowvendra Shekhar at GALF 2015").

His second work *The Adivasi Will Not Dance* is a collection of ten short stories, eight of which were published earlier in different periodicals with other titles. Each story discusses the problems faced by the Santhals in general and women in particular, as if giving an impression that the author took a particular issue and made a story out of that. The characters in each story is defined by their problem or at sometimes, the characters become nothing more than their problems ("*The Adivasi Will Not Dance* | Book Chat!"). The stories were said to be influenced by Hansda's job ("In Conversation with HansdaSowvendra Shekhar at GALF 2015"). During the book launch of *The Adivasi Will Not Dance*, Hansda was introduced as a writer who follows the style of James Arther Baldwin, who, through his works reflected the complexities of racial, sexual and class distinction and "that is the category we must look at while considering Sowvendra's works" ("Book Launch: *The Adivasi Will Not Dance* by Hansda Sowvendra Shekhar"). Through the book, the author introduced life, culture, tradition, religious views, food, folklore, land, and language that are the part and parcel of the Santhals. He explores the dreadful nature of the sufferings of Santhals, using powerful language that evokes fear, helplessness and aversion in the readers. One of the readers of the book reviewed it as a book that left a bad taste on her mouth for it has a lot of explicit contents, especially when it comes to sexual intercourse, that she was not warned about ("*The Adivasi Will Not Dance*| Book Chat!").

One cannot ignore the elements reflecting marginalisation faced by the Adivasis in general while reading Sowvendra's books. But apart from that, they discuss some other issues that the Santhals, especially those the Santhal women face. In addition to that he traces the history of the formation of a separate land for the Adivasis and how they lost it to the coal mining companies through his works. Let us discuss each of those themes.

Unfolding History

Hansda's *The Mysterious Ailment of Rupi* Baskey that revolves around the life of RupiBaskey and her family, is a novel based on an incident that took place in his village. ("In Conversation with Hansda Sowvendra Shekhar at GALF 2015"). It also provides a brief history of the creation of Jharkhand in its fourth chapter ("Lit for Life 2015:

The Hindu Prize 2014 Shortlist Reading"). The history of Jharkhand, as unfolded by the author, goes on like this:

> There was excitement and promise in the air. In Chakuliya, wherever Della and Putki went, people said that the country was free. They said that the Ingrez had left and that the sarkar would be run by our own people. Much more exciting than national freedom was the prospect of a separate land for the hor people, for the Adivasis… wherever Santhal men and women gathered, they could hear the name of Jaipal Singh… a Munda from Khunti in Ranchi…. Singh founded the Adivasi Mahasabha in 1938 which demanded a separate state called Jharkhand for the Adivasis of Chota Nagpur region. The Adivasi Mahasabha was renamed the Jharkhand Party after Independence…. Jharkhand, the hihiri-pipiri, the utopia which the Adivasis of the Chota Nagpur region had been striving for so long seemed within reach, like a ripe guava hanging from the lowermost branch of a tree, brought down low by its own weight. Just stand on your toes, stretch your arm and pluck it. ("An extract from "The Mysterious Ailment of Rupi Baskey"")

By this, he laid the background for his writings which has Jharkhand as its setting. In addition to telling stories about the Santhals, Sowvendra continued to narrate the story of Jharkhand from its birth up to its adulthood, its different stages of 'growth and development' through the later works.

Patriarchal Domination and Objectification of the Female Body as an Object of Pleasure

There are a lot of references in Sowvendra's stories, which were set in a patriarchal society, in which one can find the objectification of the human body, especially that of the female body. One can find women, and even girls, surrendering themselves as sexual toys for the satisfaction of the sexual needs of men of different ages and those who belong to different social and economic strata. In the third chapter, we can find Talamai, a girl of twenty years, selling her body for food and money to a jawan of the Railway Protection Force. When he asked Talamai whether she would "do some work" (Shekhar 40) for him, she understood the kind of work he was talking about:

> She has done it a few times by the Koyla Road, where many Santhal women and girls steal coal from trucks. She knows many girls who do that work with truck drivers and other men. And she knows

that on their way to Namal, Santhal women do this work for food and money at the railway station, too. (40)

We can find instances of patriarchal domination in this story. Thalamai, since she "knows the routine" did nothing, but "only spread her legs and lie quiet. She knows: everything is done by the man" (41) during sexual intercourse. After the "work" was done, the jawan gave Talamai two pieces of cold bread pakora and a fifty rupee note, and went away. The picture of Talamai re-tieing her saya and lungi and keeping the fifty rupee note into her blouse reflects how ignorant she is to be submissive and think that it is her duty to satisfy the needs of the so called 'powerful' ones. She eats both the bread pakoras and walks back to her group.

Another incident reflecting the objectification of women can be seen in the story "Get Even", the story that is built on the issues of the selling of Santhal girls. The unnamed narrator narrates an incident that took place in a hospital which is situated, in his own words, in a "godforsaken district in the Santhal Pargana" (43), where he works. One day a group of people and some police officers brought a ten year old boy, who was accused of having raped a girl of four years, with them. They were followed by the boy's parents who were later revealed to be in rivalry with the girl's family. As the story proceeds, it has become clear that the boy's mother was who was a member of the girl's family, who were Santhals, got converted to Christianity. Those Santhals, in the boy's father's words, were taking revenge upon the woman who left their family to live with that man who is a Hindu. They once kidnapped the fifteen-year-old elder daughter of the couple by promising her that they will provide her with a lot of money. She then left with them, and later informed her parents when she sensed the dangers awaiting her. He also added that those people were rich and they took Santhal girls from villages by making them believe that they would give them education, training, and work and then sell them away. Finally, the boy's father asked the narrator to help his family.

The explicit references to the attitude of seeing everything as objects for sale can be seen in the story titled, "Merely a Whore", in which the title reflects how patriarchy sees women as insignificant. The story is set in a coal-mining village of Lakkhipur district. While describing the place, the narrator clearly says "Everything is on sale here: bodies, companionship. All one needs to do is to keep paying" (144). There is a brothel house in that town where the central character of the story lives along with many other women. In order to bring in a comparison between Sona and the other girls there, the narrator attemptsa comparison between how they do their duties, which is to feed their belly with food, cover their body with clothes, and provide them money. He says, "Sona, the brightest star of Jharna-dhi's house. Sona was a dream; everyone else was merely a whore. The others would just spread their legs and their work was done. Sona would unlock the very gates of a palace of pleasures and invite her customers within as honoured guests" (145). Sona's worth is valued on the basis of how well she works as an object that provides a man with sexual pleasure. The narrator makes two comparisons at two different occasions to make the reader understand what made the clients prefer to have Sona over other girls. Sona being the "fresh meat" can "always attract more flies" (146) and "she was like potter's clay in their (her clients') hands" (149). There are references in this story to Sona as a "gift" (148), and a "present" (154) for she, or more precisely her body is the gift that the DySP and Nirmal received when they helped the mine owners and friend respectively. These incidents made Jharnadhi, the owner of the brothel house, believe that "as long as she had Sona, she would keep reaping profits" (148). Once she lined up the girls in front of the client and said, "Pick an item", (153) neither the clients nor Jharnadhi saw themas human beings.

One of the customer's words when Sona refused to be with men except Nirmal tells us how men consider themselves superior to women and how men see women as toys in their hands. He said, "'More new girls are coming to Lakkhipur, Jharnamaydum… men like us don't have to go looking for girls. We keep one on each finger of ours. If your Sona thinks that one of us is going to marry her and take her away somewhere, then…'" (160), giving us an impression that a man can 'choose and use' a girl and she is not expected to have a thought that he will take her away with him, no matter how well he treats her.

After breaking Sona's heart by showering abuses on her, Nirmal visited Jharna-dhi's brothel along with Nandu, a few days before Nirmal's marriage. When the girls were made to stand before them, Nirmal chose Tina, a new inmate, without even looking at Sona. It was Nandu who chose Sona (168). He told her that he missed her a lot and a lot more things, which were not heard by Sona who "just wrapped her legs around Nandu's hips and countered his thrusts. That made him happy" (168).

A girl's inability to find a suitor when she reaches a particular age is seen as a fault. There exist different notions in a patriarchal society that prevent a girl from having a suitor. One among such notions is that a woman who had undergonesexual harassment becomes impure, thus making it difficult for her to find a husband. The words by Sulochana, a character in the story, "Eating with the Enemy" resonate the same idea. When she feared whether her daughter, Mathabhangi had undergone molestation, she said, "I don't know what will happen to my daughter now. Who will marry her? Her life has been spoilt" (80). On the contrary, we find Mathabhangi's life, brimming with possibilities, changing her to be a different person after the sexual harassment. She fell in love with Chunu, her sister Seethamatha's brother-in-law, whom she married later, making her mother sigh "Didi, I am dead!... My daughter… has married that good-for-nothing Chunu" (82).

Another belief is that a girl needs to be beautiful in order to attract men. We find Bijoya, "a Santhal woman of marriageable age" (118) who was set apart from other girls in the village on the basis of her education. Even though she is a graduate and is a girl with aspirations, we find her failing to find a man to marry her for "Santhal men go for looks. While Bijoya's gold medal could get her a job, when it came to marriage negotiations, it intimidated suitors" (118).

Another story titled "Desire, Divination, Death" shares an incident in which we find people bringing women of the family to abuse someone, stilltreating men with utter reverence. Both these characteristic features or flaws of the society are shown through two different times in the life of a woman named Subhashini. On one occasion, we find Subhashini responding to a boy who shouted improper things to her, "'*Morbek tor ma*'" (133). Later, we find her regretting her action when she had thoughts like "She had done the right thing by cursing that woman. But what was that woman's fault? It was her son who had shouted at her, and made fun of her" (134). This same Subhashini refused to call her son by his own name. Kunaram, "for that was the name of her father-in-law and no good, respectable Santhal woman should bring the names of her husband, her father-in-law and her elder brother-in-law on her lips" (135). Instead, she called her son *ba, beta,* or *Kunu* when her husband called him *ba*. These two instances reflect the image of the society that treats men with utter reverence and women with negligence.

Nature, Environment, and Transformation of Villages

Sowvendra's books are mirrors placed in front of the habitat of the Santhals. He gives vivid descriptions of the environment by describing the forests, rivers, ponds and other natural resources. He who tracesthe history of the formation of Jharkhand, the separate state for Adivasis, and gives an account of the gradual transformation of its villages into coal mining towns. The fourth story in *The Adivasi Will Not Dance* gives a glimpse of Sarjomdih, a place in Jharkhand:

> Sarjomdih, which for about sixty years, was another nondescript dot on a map. That part of the Chottanagpur area which is now formally known as the PurbiSingbhum district. Sarjomdih, where most of the population is Santhal and the rest are Munda; ...Sarjomdih, whose men were given jobs as unskilled labourers in the mines and the factory in return for their fecund land. Sarjomdih, which is a standing testimony to the collapse of an agrarian Adivasi society and the dilution of Adivasi culture, the twin gifts of industrialisation and progress. (114)

This reference to the collapse of an agrarian society, keeping it under the shadow of 'development and progress' can be seen in different stories throughout the book. When people found that some coal buried under the soil, the zamindars sold their properties to mining firms and shifted to cities to live in apartments. Then the farmers were forced to desert the fields and move away, leading to the transformation of the colony of the outcastes into red-light districts.

The transformation of a Santhal village into an industrial township is described with much clarity in these words: "Villages fell, a town rose: Lakkhipur, the coal mine town. Mud houses fell, concrete ones mushroomed: roads, police outposts, a railway station, a bus depot, shops, market, a slum and the busiest red light area in the whole of the mining zone" (147). This inturn led to the transformation of farmers into coal-mining workers and the dancers of the colony of outcastes into prostitutes (146). A reference to this transformation can be seen in "Merely a Whore!". "What Jharna, and other dancing girls like her would have to do with just one man, they were forced to do with many men several times a day once the mines began operations. The musicians who once accompanied them during their performances became their pimps." (147). The impact of the end of an agrarian society and the sprouting of industrialisation can be seen in other stories in the book as well as in otherworks. In "My Father's Garden", there is a transformation of the narrator's father's happiness into grief when he has to suffer hisuncle's act of cutting down and selling the sal trees that he had nurtured.

A story in *The Adivasi Will Not Dance* under the same title is narrated by a musician named Mangal Murmu who presents himself as a person who was a farmer. He, along with the members of his troupe, were invited to perform in front of the President of India, for which they travelled from Jharkhand to Delhi. But when the time came for them to perform, Murmu refused to dance and raised a few questions to the President and the people gathered there. References to each and every theme discussed by Sowvendra in his entire work can be heard again when we listen to the questions of Murmu. He speaks helplessly about the farmlands acquired by coal merchants and the stone merchants, poverty and lack of nutrition leading to diseases, people denying them education or forcing them to worship Jesus and Mary instead of Bonga-Buru, people commanding them what to eat and what not to eat (172-173). He also adds how coal mining has affected their environment, "There is a blackness…. The trees and shrubs in our village bear black leaves. Our ochre earth has become black. The stones, the rocks, the sand, all black. The tiles on the roofs of our huts have lost their fire-burnt red…. Our children – dark skinned as they are – are forever covered with fine black dust" (175). He even mourns the absence of a leader to lead them, and the ill fate of those who tried to protest, saying, "And we Santhals? Our men are beaten up, thrown into police lock-ups, into jails, for flimsy reasons, and on false charges. Our women are raped, some sell their bodies on Koyla Road. Most of us are fleeing our places of birth. How united are we? Where are our Santhal leaders?" (176).

Pointing out these sufferings faced and still facing by the Adivasis, the story, "The Adivasi Will Not Dance" and thus the entire book ends with the words "How can we Adivasis dance and be happy? Unless we are given back our homes and land, we will not sing and dance. We Adivasis will not dance. The Adivasi will not …". These words discussing the age-old crisis of the loss of the homeland remind us of the last lines of the poem "We Are Going" (1964) by the Australian Aboriginal poet, Oodgeroo Noonuccal: "The bora ring is gone./ The corroboree is gone. And we are going" (Noonuccal) and the lamentations of the Israelites in a foreign land ("Psalm 137").

In conclusion, we can say that, even thoughwe have gained independence, there are a lot of people who are the victims of what Frantz Fanon in his *The Wretched of the Earth* calls 'neocolonialism' (colonisation laid by the powerful upper castes upon the powerless lower caste people) after decolonisation. (Originally the word 'neocolonialism', coined by Kwame Nkrumah, "describes the influence of the former imperial nations on the ex-colonies in the areas of economy, language, culture, and political philosophy." (Nwachuku)). Considering this, they belong to "nowhere". Sowvendra through his works has tried to bring to light the sufferings of a community that remained unheard and unseen for decades. The themes that he discusses through his works are woven together, which can be brought together under the umbrella of marginalisation and suffering faced by the Santhals.

Works Cited

"Ambedkar, B. R.". Encyclopedia.com. https://www.encyclopedia.com/environment/encyclopedias-almanaca-transcripts-and-maps/ambedkar-b-r. 2019. Web. 12 Aug. 2021.

Anand, Mulk Raj. *Untouchable*. New Delhi: Dorling Kindersley (India) Pvt, Ltd., licensees of Pearson Education in South Asia, 2013 Print.

"An extract from 'The Mysterious Ailment of RupiBaskey'". *issuu*. Aleph Book Company. https://issuu.com/alephbookscompany/docs/rupi_baskey. 8 Jan. 2014. Web. 2 Sep. 2021.

AzhakiyaRavanan (Malayalam). Directed by Kamal, Performances by Mammootty, Bhanupriya and Biju Menon. 9 Feb. 1996.

"Book Launch: *The Adivasi Will Not Dance* by HansdaSowvendra Shekhar". *YouTube*, uploaded by icggoa. https://youtu.be/nguxln-kQSE. 15 Jan. 2016. Web. 14 Aug. 2021.

Datta, Sudipta. "Who is HansdaSowvendra Shekhar, fighting a ban". *The Hindu*. https://www.thehindu.com/news/national/hansda-sowvendra-shekharfighting-a-ban/article19525262.ece. 19 Aug. 2017. Web. 31 Aug. 2021.

Fanon, Frantz. *The Wretched of the Earth*. New York: Grove Press, 1963. Print.

"In Conversation with HansdaSowvendra Shekhar at GALF 2015". *YouTube*, uploaded by icggoa. https://youtu.be/51FRvqMUMrY. 19 Feb. 2016. Web. 14 Aug. 2021.

"Issue Brief: Poverty and Social Exclusion in India | Adivasis". World Bank Document. https://openknowledge.worldbank.org/bitstream/handle/10986/26335/114157-BRI-India-PSE-Adivasis-Brief-PUBLIC.pdf?sequence=1. Web. 18 Aug. 2021

Keats, John. "Ode to Nightingale". Immortal Poems of the English Language. USA: Simon & Schuster. July 1952. Print.

Kumar, Aswani. "5 Banned Indian Books That You Must *not* Read". *YouTube*, uploaded by Books on Toast. https://youtu.be/-sOhrd33SwE. 28 Sep. 2018. Web. 14 Aug. 2021.

"Lit for Life 2015: The Hindu Prize 2014 Shortlist Reading". *YouTube*, Uploaded by The Hindu. https://youtu.be/1wGKxQuxWiQ. 3 Mar. 2015. Web. 2 Sep. 2021

Noonuccal, Oodgeroo. "We Are Going". *Global Voices and Cultures*. Delhi: Oxford University Press. 2021. Print.

Nwachuku, Levi A. "Neo-colonialism". Wiley Online Library. *The Encyclopedia of Empire*. https://onlinelibrary.wiley.com/doi/abs/10.1002/9781118455074.wbeoe237. 11 Jan. 2016. Web. 15 Aug. 2021

Poyam, Akash. "Ten voices from Adivasi literature". *The Caravan*. https://caravanmagazine.in/books/reading-list-ten-voices-adivasi-literature. 15 Jan. 2021. Web. 18 Aug. 2021.

"Psalm 137". *Good News Bible: Today's English Version*. Bangalore: The Bible Society of India. 1996. Print.

Shafak, Elif. *The Forty Rules of Love*. New Delhi: Thomson Press India Ltd. 2010. Print.

Shankar, Pooja. "Voices Unheard: Tribal Literature from India to Read Now". *WWB Daily*. Words without Borders: The Online Magazine for International Literature. https://wordswithoutborders.org/dispatches/article/voices-unheard-tribal-literature-from-india-to-read-now. 29 Mar. 2017. Web. 19 Aug. 2021

Shekhar, HansdaSowvendra. *The Adivasi Will Not Dance*. Noida: Shree MaitreyPrintechPvt. Ltd. 2017. Print.

.... Queries regarding *The Adivasi Will Not Dance*. AneeshyaSuprabha Michael. Sep. 2021. Email Interwiew

Tharoor, Sasi. Indian Literature: I will live... [but oppressed/repressed/depressed/suppresses]!.*Facebook*, 3 Aug. 2021, https://www.facebook.com/134735138166/posts/10158778671663167/?app=fbl. 8 Aug. 2021.

"*The Adivasi Will Not Dance* By HansdaSowvendra Shekhar || Review || Santhal Tribe Stories". *YouTube*, Uploaded by Into the Bookworld. https://youtu.be/ptS-U-Uw1lc. 7 Dec. 2020. Web. 16 Aug. 2021.

"*The Adivasi Will Not Dance* | Book Chat!". *YouTube*, Uploaded by Godhashri Reads. https://youtu.be/F-MoPc782-M. 25 Mar. 2020. Web. 31 Aug. 2021

"What is India's Caste System?". *BBC*.https://www.bbc.com/news/world-asia-india-35650616, 19 June 2019. Web. 1 July 2021.

CHAPTER 15

Tishani Doshi: A Subtle Yet Distinctive Voice in Contemporary Indian English Literature

Keerthana Raj

Indian English literature as a genre has achieved canonical heights in the contemporary literary sphere and during the recent decades it has garnered a wide spread interest both in India and abroad. The diverse yet complex and multi-faceted realities of the land, accord the writers with an opportunity to delve deep into its myriad faces. Indian English writers, especially women writers in the present day have been vocal in projecting the true Indian reality and exposed the issues prevalent in the society with a laudable courage and strength. Their intense and scintillating expressions encapsulated the hopes and traumas of a generation and played a pivotal role in bringing in the conflict-ridden structures to the forefront for negotiation and rectification. In such a promising horizon we have writers like Tishani Doshi who are adept in disrupting the stillness laden in a problematic framework. Doshi courageously takes up themes that are often pushed to the periphery and her poetry and prose is an ode to the voiceless people around the world.

The writer is an activist, dancer and freelance journalist based in Chennai. She was born on 9 December 1975 in Madras, India to Welsh-Gujarathi parents and spent her formative years in Madras, a city to which she is eternally bonded to. Doshi pursued Business Administration and Communications at Queens College, North Carolina and did her Master's degree in Creative Writing from Johns Hopkins University, Baltimore. In 1999, she shifted to London taking up the post of an assistant to the advertisement department of Harper's and Queen magazine. In 2001 she relocated to India and was drawn by the charisma of dancer Chandralekha who opened new doors to Doshi's ingenious creativity. "It was with her I began to feel an artist's life", She quotes about her mentor. Her major works include Countries of the Body [2006] which won the Foreword Poetry Prize, Conflict and Instability [2008, a collection of poems which is a joint effort of Doshi with Tobias Hill and Aoife Mannix], The Pleasure Seekers [2010, fiction], Everything Begins Elsewhere [2012, poetry collection], Fountainville [2013, Fiction], Madras Then, Chennai Now [2013, Book written in collaboration with Nanditha Krishna], The Adulterous Citizen: Poems, Stories, Essays [2015], Girls are Coming Out of the Woods [2017, Poetry Collection], Small Days and Nights [2019, Fiction] and the recently published A God at the Door [2021, Poetry Collection]. Doshi is admired for her acute, unapologetic and vigorous tone. She is also a contributing author to various reputed newspapers like The Guardian, New Express and The National. Doshi is an avid traveller who divides her time between her home by the sea in Paramankeni and elsewhere.

The Magic and Melancholy of Being 'Elsewhere': Discerning the Psyche of Immigrants in the Writings of Tishani Doshi

"[T]he diasporic space [is] the quintessential late 20th-century space, a space in which the terms of modern immigration, exile, loss, nation, subject and citizen are negotiated and reinvented for various uses."

There is something confounding to the feeling of being in a place and not being there. This kind of spiritual and geographical dislocation preoccupies the core of immigrant writings in literature. An immigrant is a person who has left his or her home country and has settled in a foreign land. The immigration experience is long and composite and has often paved paths for the creation and development of multicultural societies and ethnicities. The complex interplay involved in the process of immigration leads to cultural bereavement, identity crisis, alienation, and a staunch sense of non-belongingness. In the immigrant space, home is a mythical place of desire and those who are away from their homeland nurtures a collective memory of it. This feeling to get back to one's homeland emboldens people to maintain their relationship with their ancestral roots, thus forging a type of ancestral impulse. In fact, a majority of these immigrant communities defy the foisting of the hegemonising colonial concoct of ethnicity. This ethnic label, while it divides the different minority groups against one another to expedite the preservation of the interests of the ruling elite, also reiterates the presumption that ethnic communities do not belong here, that they belong 'elsewhere'. As Ien Ang quotes:

> "The very name with which the "ethnic" is referred to……Chinese [or Indian].. already transposes her or him to, and conjures up the received memory of, another site of symbolic belonging, a site which is not "here".

The nation/state has reinforced the homeland myth entrenched in the popular imagination, to divide and ethnicize the cultural and political landscape. In the contemporary Indian English diasporic space, we have authors especially women who are capable of drawing parallels between varied cultures and experiences. In this propitious scenario we can locate Tishani Doshi successfully thriving on her writings of loss, longing and memories. The fragmented journeys that she had embarked in life along with the immigrant memories that stay undiluted in her inner recesses help Doshi to colour the landscape of her imagination. She says:

> "It makes me stand out as an outsider, look in as an insider and gives me the power as a writer". She wove her own version of her parent's life story, one that of a reverse migration in her debut novel 'The Pleasure Seekers'. In the boldly drawn generational saga characterised by wit and humour, we find Babo Patel, a young Indian of Gujarathi descend from Madras flying to London in pursuit of dreams. Babo's acculturation in the English society which has a tinge of racial prejudices is comparatively less traumatic as he had strong grounding in English language that made his adaptation much easier and fast. This is because language and behavioural assimilation occur immediately after immigrants' arrival in the host country, as they grapple with communicating in the new language and accommodating to behavioural norms and expectations in the foreign society. However, other facets of cultural change such as identity or values are thought to come later. In London, Babo meets the beautiful gap-toothed girl Sian Jones from North Wales and fell for her. The cross-cultural love of the couple invites cultural shock and dismay of the parents. After much hesitancy, the lovers are finally allowed to marry, with Sian taking a bold decision to uproot to India leaving behind Wales with its meagre and ancient light. Sian, brimming with doubts and hopes settle in India as Babo's bride and she transition from a Western girl to an Indian involved several rites of passage which she does with utmost integrity. The psyche of an immigrant who migrates for marriage or employment can be more flexible as compared to other categories of immigrants whose migrations were daunted by force, for instance, the refugees. In her host patriarchal family in madras, Sian was trained to be an Indian woman wearing a saree, looking after domestic chores. Sian's connections with external society, forging spiritual and social bonds helped her to integrate with her chosen culture.

> "But then, she believed that she had learnt the secret of surviving in a foreign country. It had something to do with love [Doshi,154].

Sian, however was skeptical about the fate of her bi-racial children, about the pangs and displaced angst that they might succumb to in their lives. Their children Mayuri and Bean had contradictory mental structures. While the elder Mayuri settles for a wedded life with a Parsi boy in India conforming her ability to survive in a multicultural environment, Bean leaves for England seeking love and adventure. About the decision of their two children, Babo comments:

> "Perhaps it's inevitable, Babo thought that our children suffer a similar displacement; that in order to understand the pattern of their lives here, they must go elsewhere.... [Doshi,236]

Bean scuffled with her disjunctured identity all throughout her life and becomes a perpetually rootless person. She introspects:

> "Is this my real life or is it just a prelude to something before I return .... Return to where? Why do I always feel like I'm visiting wherever I go? One foot in, the other foot out" [Doshi,248]. For a diasporic like Bean "There is no such thing as home. Once you've forsaken it and stepped out of the circle, you can't ever re-enter and claim anything as yours" [Doshi,278]. For Tishani Doshi, this is a novel that sprouts from life, a tender love story of desire, independence and choices.

Doshi's poetry collection 'Everything Begins Elsewhere' is a profound meditation on dreams and memories, on the art of losing and reclamation. "If we understood loss better perhaps we could accept it better, and understand loss and reclamation are opposite sides of the same coin" says Tishani Doshi. Her poems steer us through an underworld of longing and deliverance where only through the art of vanishing can we be shaped into existence again. Her poem 'Adulterous Citizen' from the collection offers poignant sense of a space and time that you can embrace but cannot call as one's own. It inexorably takes us to the realm of loss and longing. The acute agony of non-belongingness is tangible in her prose because she herself had carried the vehement sense of a citizen in exile and dreamed of a city while being in the pleasure and pathos of the other. Here she traverses back and forth to past, present and future and often transcends the metaphysical boundaries of it through her potent poetical sense.

> "that you can always return like this-
> Without key in hand,
> to lie in the folds of one city,

While listening to the jagged,
Carnal breaths of another."

Another poem from the collection titled 'The Immigrant's Song' stands apart for its highly suggestive and evocative imagery employed. Doshi herself being an immigrant tries to recapture and celebrate the resilience and ethos of an immigrant and also empathizes with them while doing so. The immigrants who are victims of a traumatic past are trying to erase the memories of days when they wished for war to end, when the headscarves of their mothers hung like white flags in hope and desperation. The poet emphasizes the necessity to elude one's unlighted past by repeating the phrase 'let us not speak of those days' because the cataclysmic events of gone days have the power to shatter one's present and future. The disturbing images of loss and abandonment should be outstripped for remembering them will not bring them back. The memories of certain fond images and scents that are entwined in the hearts of immigrants can potentially evoke an acute sense of nostalgia which can lead to a painful longing and it reinforces their own diasporic reality. Hence there is an essential need to relish the new found horizons of the host land offering a better life and to incorporate with the host culture so as to lessen the sense of estrangement perceived in an alien land. Also, Doshi does not advocate a complete silence or pause to the tales that the immigrant has in their hearts engraved. The immigrants song should be passed down from generations to generations like an oral folklore being transmitted challenging and transcending the corporal realities.

A similar sense of grief and humiliation can be discerned in the poetry of Imtiaz Dharker who was also familiar with the trauma of an immigrant. Through her poem 'The Minority' she exposed the marginalisation she endured in a foreign land while struggling with feelings of alienation and rootlessness. She laments;

"I was born a foreigner.
I carried on from there
to become a foreigner everywhere".

The disturbing, almost palpable sense of unsettlement is evident when she says:

"I don't fit,
like a clumsily-translated poem;"

Doshi's recent novel 'Small Days and Nights' pricks us with a notion of weariness and unbelongingness. Her protagonist Grace who is a half-Indian and half-Italian American immigrant is propelled to return to India following the death of her mother and to revamp her family back in India. The undercurrents caused by duality are tangible in the novel as Grace explains to her estranged husband: 'I try to explain what it means to live two lives, two inhabit two different spaces'. Doshi portraits the essence of duality as something that broadens imagination rather than restricting it. However, in this process she doesn't undermine the bruises that being an outsider can sometimes bring. Like Doshi who has relocated her life to a small coastal village called Paramankeni, her heroine Grace also inherits a house by the beach from her mother and is being bewitched by the beauty and perils of life in an unknown remote coastal village at times bearing the burden of wanting to be wherever she is not.

Tishani Doshi's writings are inevitably an exploration of what it means to be a writer in times of changing identities and displacements. For Doshi the idea of home is always a fragile one, constantly shifting and taking different forms and feelings. She finds enthrallment in the interplay of having to navigate through a space where she lives but cannot claim one's own, finds euphoria in the magic and melancholy of being 'elsewhere'.

Work Cited

Doshi, Tishani. *Everything Begins Elsewhere.* Harper Collins, India, 2012.

Doshi, Tishani. *The Pleasure Seekers.* 2nd ed., Bloomsbury, London, 2010.

Doshi, Tishani. *Small Days And Nights.* Bloomsbury, London, 2019.

Ang, Ien. *On Not Speaking Chinese: Living Between Asia and the West.* Routledge London, 2001.

Batra Jagdish. "Tishani Doshi's The Pleasure Seekers: Exploring Limits of Acculturation." *Psychology and Education Journal,* von.58.no.4, 2021, pp.1442-1452. Scopus.

Krumrey, Diane. "Displacing the Nation: Contemporary Literature by and about Immigrants." *Caliban French Journal of English Studies,* Vol.19.2006, pp.243-252., directory of Open Access Journals.

Okwui, Enwezor. "A Question of Place: revisions, reassessments, diaspora." *Smithsonian Libraries African Art Index,* Vol.6768.1997, pp.80-88. Smithsonian Libraries:

Sriram, Aditi. "In South India, a Fragmented Family Turns Into An Overflowing One." nytimes.com, *The Newyork Times,*. 22 Jan. 2020, google.com/amp/s/www.nytimes.com/2020/01/22/books/renew/small-days and-nights-tishani-doshi-amp-html/. Accessed 13 August 2021.

Lepur, Lea. "5 Fascinating Desi Poems on Immigration." Desiblitz.com, Desiblitz, 3 Sept.2018, https://www.desiblitz.com/content/fascinating-desi-poems-immgration/. Accessed 13 August 2021.

Haider, Mariyam. "The Idea of Home is always a fragile one: an interview with Tishani Doshi." asianreviewofbooks.com, *Asian Review of Books*, 20 February.2020, https://asianreviewofbooks.com/content/the-idea-of-home-is-always-a-fragile-one-an-interview-with-tishani-doshi/. Accessed 15 August 2021.

Doshi, Tishani., and James Kidd. "My Small But Relevent Paramankeni Novel." Unbound.com, Boundless, https://unbound.com/boundless/2019/06/04/we-have-the-great-calcutta-novel-the-great-delhinovel-the-small-but-relevant-paramankeni-novel/. Accessed 15 August 2021.

Bradshaw, Peter. "The Pleasure Seekers by Tishani Doshi." Theguardian.com, *The Guardian*, 21 May 2010, https://www.google.com/amp/s/ amp.theguardian.com/books/2010/may/22/pleasure-seekers-tishani-doshi/. Accessed 16 August 2021.

Index